PHONICS AND WORD IDENTIFICATION INSTRUCTION AND INTERVENTION, K–8

MARY T. RYCIK
ASHLAND UNIVERSITY

JAMES A. RYCIK
ASHLAND UNIVERSITY

Upper Saddle River, New Jersey
Columbus, Ohio

KH

Library of Congress Cataloging in Publication Data

Rycik, Mary Taylor.
  Phonics and word identification: instruction and intervention, K–8/Mary Taylor Rycik, James A. Rycik.
      p. cm.
  Includes bibliographical references and index.
  ISBN 0-13-118663-9 (alk. paper)
  1. Reading—Phonetic method. 2. Word recognition. I. Rycik, James A. II. Title.
  LB1050.34.R93 2007
  372.46'5—dc22   2005029489

Vice President and Executive Publisher: Jeffery W. Johnston
Senior Editor: Linda Ashe Montgomery
Senior Production Editor: Mary M. Irvin
Design Coordinator: Diane C. Lorenzo
Senior Editorial Assistant: Laura Weaver
Production Coordination and Text Design: Amy Gehl, Carlisle Editorial Services
Cover Designer: Candace Rowley
Cover Images: Images.com
Production Manager: Pamela D. Bennett
Director of Marketing: David Gessell
Marketing Manager: Darcy Betts Prybella
Marketing Coordinator: Brian Mounts

This book was set in Galliard by Carlisle Publishing Services. It was printed and bound by R. R. Donnelley & Sons Company. The cover was printed by R. R. Donnelley & Sons Company.

Photo Credits: All photos supplied by the authors.

Pearson Education Ltd.
Pearson Education Singapore Pte. Ltd.
Pearson Education Canada, Ltd.
Pearson Education—Japan

Pearson Education Australia Pty. Limited
Pearson Education North Asia Ltd.
Pearson Educación de Mexico, S. A. de C.V.
Pearson Education Malaysia Pte. Ltd.

10 9 8 7 6 5 4 3 2 1
ISBN: 0-13-118663-9

8/11/06

We dedicate this book to our children, Paul and Katie Rycik, who have been our best teachers of life.

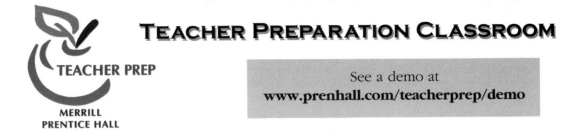

TEACHER PREPARATION CLASSROOM

See a demo at
www.prenhall.com/teacherprep/demo

YOUR CLASS. THEIR CAREERS. OUR FUTURE. WILL YOUR STUDENTS BE PREPARED?

We invite you to explore our new, innovative and engaging website and all that it has to offer you, your course, and tomorrow's educators! Organized around the major courses pre-service teachers take, the Teacher Preparation site provides media, student/teacher artifacts, strategies, research articles, and other resources to equip your students with the quality tools needed to excel in their courses and prepare them for their first classroom.

This ultimate on-line education resource is available at no cost, when packaged with a Merrill text, and will provide you and your students access to:

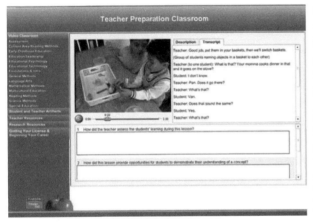

Online Video Library. More than 150 video clips—each tied to a course topic and framed by learning goals and Praxis-type questions—capture real teachers and students working in real classrooms, as well as in-depth interviews with both students and educators.

Student and Teacher Artifacts. More than 200 student and teacher classroom artifacts—each tied to a course topic and framed by learning goals and application questions—provide a wealth of materials and experiences to help make your study to become a professional teacher more concrete and hands-on.

Research Articles. Over 500 articles from ASCD's renowned journal *Educational Leadership*. The site also includes Research Navigator, a searchable database of additional educational journals.

Teaching Strategies. Over 500 strategies and lesson plans for you to use when you become a practicing professional.

Licensure and Career Tools. Resources devoted to helping you pass your licensure exam; learn standards, law, and public policies; plan a teaching portfolio; and succeed in your first year of teaching.

How to ORDER Teacher Prep for you and your students:
For students to receive a *Teacher Prep* Access Code with this text, instructors **must** provide a special value pack ISBN number on their textbook order form. To receive this special ISBN, please email **Merrill.marketing@pearsoned.com** and provide the following information:
- Name and Affiliation
- Author/Title/Edition of Merrill text

Upon ordering Teacher Prep for their students, instructors will be given a lifetime *Teacher Prep* Access Code.

PREFACE

Educators have been debating about the best way to teach reading for as long as children have been attending school. The so-called "reading wars" have pitted those arguing for an emphasis on systematic instruction in letters and sounds against those with a more holistic view of reading. In this book, we take a broad view of phonics that includes both readers' knowledge about letters, sounds, and words and their ability to use that knowledge to construct meaning. We see phonics as one very important part of word identification, and word identification as one very important part of reading. We also believe, however, that the goal of teaching phonics and word identification is to create fluent, independent readers who can comprehend, not just students who can "sound out" words.

Phonics instruction is generally associated with beginning reading instruction, but readers continue to learn how to use their knowledge about letters, sounds, and word structures well into the middle grades and beyond. This is particularly true for those students with learning disabilities and those who are English language learners. Throughout this book, we will highlight some of the factors that may cause readers to struggle and present a wide range of intervention strategies to assist them.

Phonics and Word Identification: Instruction and Intervention, K–8 is designed to address the needs of students from kindergarten to eighth grade and includes instructional activities for typical learners as well as interventions for students who may be struggling. It describes current research that informs instruction and assessment of phonics and word identification on all levels of reading development. It also provides examples of how research findings can be applied in actual classrooms.

SPECIAL FEATURES

Every chapter in this text:

- Begins with a vignette that presents either a classroom scenario or a glimpse into the classroom drawn from our own observations and interviews with teachers. Questions are provided for prereading discussion and to guide the reader's understanding. These opening classroom scenarios are then used as examples throughout the chapter. Each chapter includes research-based, teacher-tested practical activities that provide key pedagogy elements for teaching phonics and word identification.

- Includes *Interventions When Students Struggle*. This feature provides descriptions of various kinds of special needs, such as learning disabilities and developmental delays, and the effect they have on students' abilities to use phonics and word identification. Practical, research-based interventions are then described, and glimpses inside intervention classrooms are given.

- Provides an assessment feature that guides the reader to provide authentic, informal assessment of phonemic awareness, consonants, vowels, spelling, and affixes.

- Ends with a set of activities called *Before You Move On*. These include reviews of key terms and the feature *What's in This Chapter for Me?* that relates the material in the chapter to the needs of teachers in early childhood and middle grades and intervention specialists.

- Highlights key vocabulary and frequently illustrates instructional practices by text boxes or photographs. It also provides extensive lists of useful resources, including children's literature and Internet sites.

CONTENT AND ORGANIZATION

Chapter 1: Phonics: What, Why, and How? examines multiple definitions of phonics and discusses how phonics relates to word identification and to reading. The historical context of the "reading wars" is explained, and the more recent effects of the National Reading Panel and the No Child Left Behind legislation are described. The role of phonics and word identification is also discussed with regard to reading instruction for middle grades and with struggling readers.

Chapter 2: Making Decisions About Instruction: What Teachers Need to Know provides an overview of phonics and word identification by highlighting basic information that all reading teachers should have. This includes information about cueing systems, graphemes and phonemes, the stages of word learning, alphabetic and letter knowledge, and phonemic awareness. Intervention for students with learning disabilities and assessment of phonemic awareness are stressed. The key features of different approaches to teaching phonics and word identification are also presented.

Chapter 3: Learning and Teaching About Consonants builds on the readers' understanding of phonemes and graphemes as they apply to consonants and consonant clusters. The most common sound-symbol relationships are presented, as well as exceptions to these. Numerous suggestions for teaching and assessing consonants are described.

Chapter 4: Learning and Teaching About Vowels presents information about the variety of vowel sounds and patterns in the English language. Spelling patterns that tend to produce short and long vowel sounds are introduced.

Vowel diphthongs, vowel digraphs, controlled vowels, and schwa sounds are also thoroughly explained. Vowel rimes (the vowel and the rest of the syllable) that are common for each of these vowel combinations are also listed. This chapter also includes teaching strategies that actively involve students in using onsets and rimes. Interventions for students with reading delays are featured and an easy-to-use informal assessment of vowel sounds is given.

Chapter 5: Incorporating Phonics and Word Identification into Reading Instruction explores the best ways to teach phonics and word identification within a meaningful context. These include shared reading with Big Books, poetry and verse, use of literature circles, and guided reading instruction. The controversy over decodable text is examined. Assessment of word identification using running records and informal reading inventories is also discussed. A look into three different level classrooms where teachers are using these strategies is provided.

Chapter 6: Spelling and Writing Instruction provides ways of effectively teaching spelling and writing to students. For background, terms such as *orthography* and *high frequency words* are defined. The stages of spelling development are described and illustrated with actual student writing. The interpretation and misinterpretation of "invented spelling" is discussed. Classroom strategies that have been found to be effective in teaching spelling and writing are described, including shared writing, writing journals, word walls, writing workshop, and buddy spelling. Interventions for students who struggle with spelling and the assessment of spelling are featured in this chapter. In addition, easy-to-make games are included.

Chapter 7: Teaching Word Structure for Sound and Meaning focuses on the morphemic or structural analysis of words, such as analyzing prefixes, suffixes, roots, and inflectional endings that affect the meanings of words. Strategies for helping students to analyze words are presented. A simple assessment of affixes and a discussion of interventions for students who struggle with these types of words are provided. Word origins and the creation of new words are also explored.

Chapter 8: Accommodating and Supporting Students with Language Differences examines the challenges faced by students who are learning English and identifies principles and strategies for helping students learn and use new language forms. This chapter also discusses issues related to the diverse dialects and forms of English such as ebonics and suggests guidelines for giving all students equal opportunities to learn through culturally responsive instruction. Regional dialects are also explored.

ACKNOWLEDGMENTS

We wish to thank the classroom teachers, especially Katie Steffen, Teri Jewett, Donna Lanyi, Kate Blair, Denee Schlotterer, Krista Alberty, Marcia Stoffer,

Michelle Zerrer, and Monica Carrera-Wilburn for allowing us to visit their classrooms and see great instruction in phonics and word identification.

We want to thank our wonderful editor, Linda Montgomery, and her editorial assistant, Laura Weaver, as well as Amy Gehl of Carlisle Publishing Services, for all the personal attention and invaluable advice they have given us. You have helped us find our way through this process. We also want to thank all of our book reviewers who helped us to refine and improve our ideas: Patricia DeMay, University of West Alabama; Shirley B. Ernst, Eastern Connecticut State University; Ray Ostrander, Andrews University; Timothy Rasinski, Kent State University; Timothy Shanahan, University of Illinois at Chicago; and Mahmoud Suleiman, California State University, Bakersfield.

Finally, we wish to thank the students at Ashland University who used drafts of our book and gave us valuable feedback and new ideas. We hope that we have helped you to prepare for the most important job on earth: teaching.

FOREWORD

In Norton Juster's delightful book *The Phantom Tollbooth* (1961), Milo samples letters in the marketplace of Dictionopolis, the kingdom of words. He first tries an *A*:

> Milo nibbled carefully at the letter and discovered that it was quite sweet and delicious— just the way you'd expect an A to taste.
>
> "I knew you'd like it," laughed the letter man, popping two G's and an R into his mouth and letting the juice drip down his chin. "A's are one of our most popular letters. All of them aren't that good," he confided in a low voice. "Take the Z for instance—very dry and sawdusty. And the X? Why it tastes like a trunkful of stale air. That's why people hardly ever use them."

In this book, we hope to make letters and words a delicious and not the least bit stale experience.

Contents

CHAPTER 3   LEARNING AND TEACHING ABOUT CONSONANTS   35

CHAPTER 4   LEARNING AND TEACHING ABOUT VOWELS   53

CHAPTER 5   INCORPORATING PHONICS AND WORD IDENTIFICATION INTO READING INSTRUCTION   71

CHAPTER 6   SPELLING AND WRITING INSTRUCTION   89

Note: Every effort has been made to provide accurate and current Internet information in this book. However, the Internet and information posted on it are constantly changing, so it is inevitable that some of the Internet addresses listed in this text book will change.

PHONICS: WHAT, WHY, AND HOW?

D r. Taylor made eye contact with the undergraduate education majors in her freshman literacy class and asked the question again, "What is phonics?" The students, suspecting a trick question, were reluctant to answer. Justin finally raised his hand and said, "It's sounding out words, right?"

Natalie suddenly piped in, "Yeah, it's learning the sounds of the letters and then putting the sounds together to make words, like in the 'Hooked on Phonics' commercial."

"Ok," Dr. Taylor said. "You seem to agree that phonics is about how words sound, but sometimes putting all the sounds together doesn't work. Think of a word like *bright*. How can you make your definition fit those words?"

Kevin replied, "It's knowing the rules for how to pronounce the words."

"I never learned phonics," said Jennifer. "My teachers believed in whole language."

"But how are kids supposed to learn how to read if they can't figure out the words?" asked Naomi.

Dr. Taylor smiled and said, "Even experienced teachers don't always agree on what phonics is and how it should be taught, but everyone agrees it is a topic that any teacher of reading needs to know and think about."

Take a moment to think about this classroom discussion:

- With which statements are you in agreement?
- How would you define phonics?
- What other questions about phonics should teachers consider?
- Is it necessary to know phonics in order to read?
- Is phonics a methodology for teaching reading or is it one part of an overall reading program?
- Is it worthwhile to teach phonics and spelling rules when so many words are irregular?
- Why has phonics often been controversial?

Classroom teacher and educational author, Regie Routman (2000) once wrote, "Phonics is a lot like sex. Everyone is doing it behind closed doors, but no one is talking about it" (p. 91). Increasingly, however, phonics *is* being talked about, and teachers can no longer make their decisions about what and how to teach behind closed doors.

Phonics has often been at the center of a rising public debate about reading instruction that has been as much political as educational. Standards-based education, high-stakes testing, and issues related to the No Child Left Behind legislation have had a profound impact on how reading is taught in schools today.

As we talk about phonics and word identification in this chapter, we will explore different ideas about what phonics is and what role it should play in literacy instruction. We will also consider how the demands made by standards-based education and high-stakes testing can be met in a comprehensive approach to reading instruction, one in which phonics plays an important but not solitary role.

☐ DEFINING PHONICS AND WORD IDENTIFICATION

The term *phonics* has both a general meaning and a more technical meaning. When a person says that a child "doesn't know his phonics," or suggests that a student who is struggling to spell a word should "sound it out," the person is referring to the knowledge that readers and writers have about how letters and sounds correspond.

Phonics has also been defined as a method for teaching reading. In fact, *The Literacy Dictionary* (Harris & Hodges, 1995) defines phonics as "a way of teaching reading and spelling that stresses symbol–sound relationships" (p. 186). As a teaching method, phonics is described in terms of the kinds of lessons that teachers present, the sorts of assignments that they give, and sometimes the materials that they use. As you will see in this chapter, phonics as a teaching method has often been highly controversial, especially when educators, politicians, or members of the public have insisted that teachers choose between a phonics method of teaching reading and one that is opposed to phonics. We contend, however, that students can be guided to learn about sounds and words in many ways and that there is really no "non-phonics" approach to reading instruction. We also believe that phonics is used and learned in both reading and writing.

In this book we take a broad view of phonics that includes what teachers, readers, and writers do. We define **phonics** as the knowledge about letters, sounds, and words that people use to create meaning when reading and writing and the ways in which they are guided to acquire that knowledge.

At the beginning of this chapter, students in Professor Taylor's class attempted to define phonics. Consider how their responses show different aspects of our definition of phonics. Justin, for example, was repeating a common informal definition when he defined phonics as "sounding out words." Natalie added that phonics is "learning the sounds of the letters and then putting the sounds together to make words." Both were describing two essential skills of phonics: **segmenting,** or listening to the individual sounds of letters (s-a-t), and **blending,** putting those sounds together to form a whole word.

Professor Taylor expounded on an important truth, that segmenting and blending cannot be used to identify all words. For example, words such as *said, have, was,* and *love* cannot be "sounded out" letter by letter, and yet they are common words that all students must learn.

English is a complex language. Teaching phonics involves pointing out these complexities and suggesting ways for students to deal with them. As Kevin pointed out, there are "rules," even if those rules have many exceptions. Teaching phonics may include drawing attention to well-known statements, such as "*i* before *e* except after *c*," that are true often enough to be helpful to readers and writers. Rules may also be thought of as patterns that readers can use to figure out the pronunciation of similar words (Johnston, 2001). For example, the *-ate* pattern in *late* can be applied to read the words *hate, mate, Kate, date, fate.*

You might have noticed Jennifer's comment that she "never learned phonics." Jennifer could not have developed the ability to read well enough to succeed in college if she had not learned a great deal about the relationship between sounds and letters. It may have been more accurate for her to say that her teachers did not present lessons that were identified as phonics lessons.

Jennifer pointed out that her teachers believed in an approach called "whole language." The relationship between that approach and phonics will be discussed later in this chapter as we briefly trace controversies connected to phonics instruction.

Phonics is a tool for unlocking words, just as a hammer is a tool for building a house. The object of using a hammer is to build a strong house, not to become proficient at hammering, and the point of phonics is to help students become better *readers*, not better phonics users. As the title of this book indicates, we believe that phonics is closely tied to **word identification,** "the process of determining the pronunciation and some degree of meaning of an unknown word" (Harris & Hodges, 1995, p. 282).

Word identification includes not only analyzing letters and sounds, but also using context clues and knowledge of word structure. A first grader may, for instance, make the /d/ sound at the first letter of *doorbell* but also use the clue of a picture showing a person standing at a door. The sentence context that says, "Paul rang the _____" provides an additional clue to help confirm the student's choice. A third grader who knows the word *able* and uses it to figure out the name *Mrs. Arable* in a story is using knowledge about word parts as a strategy for word identification. A seventh grader who notices that the word *indisputable* incorporates the pieces *in, dispute,* and *able* shows knowledge of word structure; in the middle grades and beyond, this becomes increasingly important.

☐ PHONICS IN THE MIDDLE GRADES?

Because of the public debate about phonics for beginning reading instruction, many people think phonics and word identification are taught exclusively in the primary grades. However, readers of all ages continue to use phonics as they identify and produce written words. Throughout the intermediate and middle grades, students need to develop strategies for using the knowledge about words that they already have and for learning new word patterns.

Consider the word *plam*. You may have never seen this word before, but you did not have trouble reading it, because you consciously or unconsciously applied a word identification strategy. The letters form familiar patterns that look like words you already know, so you probably chunked this word into two parts, *pl* and *am*. You know the sound of *pl* because of the many words that begin this way, such as *play*. You are also familiar with words that have the -*am* ending chunk, such as *jam*.

Students may use some strategies easily and automatically, but they will probably need instruction about additional strategies and when to use them.

This need for guidance "is not the result of any teaching or learning failure in the preschool or primary years; it is a necessary part of normal reading development" (Moore, Bean, Birdyshaw, & Rycik, 1999, p. 4). In the middle grades, students encounter an increasing number of unfamiliar words, especially in content areas such as science, social studies, and math. Without sufficient word identification strategies, students may just skip over these words and miss an important opportunity to learn new vocabulary. Teachers, including content area teachers, must be prepared to model and support advanced word identification.

How would you help middle grade students figure out the following words?

cerebellum   photosynthesis   polygon   emancipation

You probably would not suggest letter-by-letter "sounding." Students would need to use a fairly sophisticated combination of their understanding of the subject, their ability to see meaningful chunks within the words, and their oral language knowledge.

To help all students learn, teachers in the middle grades need a thorough understanding of the patterns of sounds and letters found in English, and they need to know a variety of techniques for helping students to solve the problems they encounter when reading and writing.

☐ INTERVENTION WHEN STUDENTS STRUGGLE

Many students experience difficulties from time to time with some aspect of reading, including phonics and word identification. Teachers must know a variety of appropriate interventions—techniques for providing additional support that will allow students to move forward with their reading development. When students experience persistent difficulties, intervention specialists may help identify the cause of problems, suggest instructional approaches, or carry out appropriate interventions.

An incomplete understanding about letters and sounds often plays a role in students' struggles with reading and writing, but that does not mean that starting over with beginning phonics instruction is always an appropriate intervention. Students may need to be taught how to use sentence meaning as part of their strategy to figure out words. They may also need to increase the number of common "sight words" that they can instantly recognize. They may be guided to self-monitor by asking themselves if their reading sounds right and makes sense. All of these interventions are commonly used to help readers when they struggle. To better understand the role of phonics, it is necessary to look at the controversies in its history.

☐ THE READING WARS: THE ROLE OF PHONICS IN READING INSTRUCTION

Phonics as an instructional method has long been controversial. It has gone in and out of favor and has often been used as a political football. The ongoing debates about the role of phonics instruction have been so intense that they have sometimes been referred to as "the reading wars." Following is a brief history of phonics and reading since the end of World War II.

THE 1950S AND 1960S: THE GREAT DEBATE

In 1955, Rudolph Flesch's book, *Why Johnny Can't Read*, caused a sensation in educational circles by contending that Johnny could not read because he was not taught phonics. Flesch attacked the "look and say" method often used at the time, which had students begin to read by studying how common words looked rather than by beginning with letters and sounds. Flesch's book became a bestseller and also launched the "reading wars" that have continued on and off ever since.

In 1967, author Jean Chall attempted to settle the war over phonics with her book, *Learning to Read: The Great Debate*. After reviewing the available research on beginning reading, Chall concluded that an emphasis on phonics, or decoding, was essential. She stated, "An initial code emphasis produces better readers and spellers" (p. 84). According to Chall, research confirmed that a student's ability to recognize letters was "more essential for success in the early stages of reading than high intelligence and good oral language ability" (p. 84). Chall did not, however, settle all questions about phonics. She did not recommend one particular phonics method over another, and she pointed out that her conclusions applied only to phonics as a means for beginning reading instruction. She also cautioned that phonics instruction should not be done at the expense of other instructional practices that focused more on meaning.

At about the same time as Chall's book, Bond and Dykstra (1967) compiled *The First Grade Studies*, which examined the effectiveness of various methods of teaching beginning reading. After reviewing instructional practices in first-grade classes across the country, Bond and Dykstra concluded that no single set of instructional practices was superior. They found that phonics was an effective way to teach word identification, but they also concluded that good teachers were more important than the particular methods and materials that were used (Johnson & Baumann, 1984).

THE 1970S AND 1980S: PHONICS VERSUS COMPREHENSION

In the late 1960s and early 1970s, the great debate entered a new phase as some reading experts began raising questions about whether schools were emphasizing phonics at the expense of comprehension. Johnson and Baumann (1984) stated two major findings from research on word identification in the 1960s and 1970s: (1) Programs that emphasized phonics resulted in superior word-calling ability but not necessarily comparable comprehension skills, and (2) children displayed distinct differences in the kind of mistakes they made based on their instructional program. Barr (1972), for example, found that students taught by a phonics method produced more nonsense words than students receiving sight word instruction. When readers made mistakes that were not real words, they were assumed to be more concerned with letters and their sounds than with making sense of what they were reading. Other studies (Dank, 1976; Norton & Hubert, 1977) confirmed that students who were taught with a phonics method produced more nonword mistakes than students who were taught with basal readers that emphasized the meaning of stories. Students taught with such a "meaning-based" approach still made mistakes, but their mistakes were more likely to make sense.

In the 1980s, researchers reexamined the question of whether phonics helped or hindered comprehension. These new studies revealed a correlation between decoding ability and comprehension. Lesgold and Resnick (1982), for example, found that decoding skill accurately predicted later reading comprehension. In a longitudinal study, Juel (1988) followed a group of 54 students over several years. Juel showed that good readers on every grade level had considerably better decoding skills than poor readers. Stanovich (1991) also found the importance of word recognition as a predictor of success in comprehension:

> Since word recognition skill will be a by-product of any successful approach to developing reading ability—whether or not the approach specifically targets word recognition—lack of skill of recognizing words is always a reasonable predictor of difficulties in developing reading comprehension ability. (Stanovich, 1991, p. 418)

Even though these studies found that decoding skill was a good *predictor* of a student's ability to comprehend text, the studies did not prove that teaching phonics was the *cause* of students' good comprehension.

THE 1990S: WHOLE LANGUAGE VERSUS PHONICS

Researchers and educators had been engaged in off-and-on skirmishes about reading instruction since the end of World War II, but the great battle of the reading wars was the fierce struggle over the approach to reading instruction known as whole language. Goodman (1986) stated that whole language was based on the principles that reading is as natural a process as speaking and that it should be taught in meaningful whole contexts rather than broken down into a sequence of skill lessons and practice exercises.

Goodman emphasized that whole language was more a philosophy of teaching and learning language than a method, and teachers using whole language resisted a "cookbook" approach to teaching reading in which lessons were sequenced and scripted for them. Nevertheless, by the 1990s, a number of studies had been done comparing children in whole language classrooms with those in traditional ones. In a review of these studies, Weaver (1994) concluded that children in whole language classrooms developed better skills in phonics, vocabulary, spelling, punctuation, and grammar; that they seemed to enjoy reading more; and that they had a stronger sense of independence and identification of themselves as readers and writers (p. 323).

Sacks and Mergendoller (1997) found that reading achievement of lower scoring children improved more in kindergarten whole language classrooms than in phonics-oriented classrooms. The authors also found that students in whole language classrooms spent more time looking at books, dictating stories, and writing by using "invented" spelling than students in the phonics-oriented classes who spent more time copying words and completing worksheets.

Claims that whole language was clearly superior to phonics were countered by researchers who echoed earlier views concerning the importance of word recognition to beginning reading instruction. The work of Marilyn Adams' (1990), *Beginning to Read: Thinking and Learning About Print*, was particularly influential. In her book, Adams concluded:

> "thorough knowledge of letters, spelling patterns, and words, and of the phonological translations of all three, is vital to both skillful reading and its acquisition. Instruction designed to develop children's sensitivity to spellings and their relations to pronunciations is of paramount importance in developing proper reading skills. This is, of course, the intent of good phonics instruction" (Adams, 1990, p. 416).

Note that Adams did not prescribe a particular instructional method. She simply said that any good reading program would help readers to become more sensitive to the relationship between letters and sounds. In fact, Adams favored developing decoding and other word recognition skills during authentic reading and writing activities, which was consistent with a whole language view, and she criticized some traditional practices such as round-robin oral reading and skills worksheets.

The whole language movement in the United States came under fierce attack in 1995 when California students, who had been part of a literature-based language arts framework since 1987, scored next to last in reading proficiency among 39 states taking the National Assessment of Educational Progress test (cited in Matson, 1996). State legislators reacted by passing a law requiring that phonics be incorporated into reading instruction in California. Advocates of whole language pointed to flaws in the interpretation of the data as well as other possible explanations for poor performance in California schools, such as large class sizes and a large population of students who were English language learners (Moustafa, 1997). Some viewed the California case as largely a political attack on whole language by those with a conservative, "back to basics" agenda:

> We see this attack on curriculum as an attack on equity and democracy. Whole language, in theory and practice, holds the potential for many children to experience success. But society at large may not support universal success for children and may seek to limit who succeeds by controlling education. (Nickel & Crowley, 1999)

Whole language faced even more crises when the National Institute of Child Health and Human Development (NICHHD) attacked the concept that reading is a natural process and supported direct instruction in phonemic awareness and phonics (Lyon, 1998). The report directly attacked whole language theories about word identification: "Moreover, the view some whole language advocates hold that skilled readers gloss over the text, sampling only parts of words, and examining several lines of print to decode unfamiliar words, is not consistent with available data" (p. 17).

Some educators continued to argue that phonics and whole language were not really opposite approaches. They believed that some classroom teachers had misinterpreted whole language principles' especially by not teaching skills directly. As Early (1992–1993) put it, "I go on worrying about Whole Language teachers who neglect the direct instruction still needed by most children who are just learning to assimilate new ideas through reading" (p. 306).

Eventually, many reading educators stopped using the term *whole language* to avoid seemingly endless arguments. Stanovich (1993–1994) summed up the situation by saying, "It seems inconceivable that we will continue wasting energy on the reading wars simply because we cannot get both sides to say simultaneously, 'Some teachers overdo phonics' and 'Some children need explicit instruction in alphabetic coding'" (p. 285).

Much of the debate about phonics instruction has tended to suggest that phonics must either be "first and most" or "last and least." The term **balanced literacy** has been suggested as an alternative that promotes "common sense and common ground" (Rycik, 1997). Strickland (1998) described balanced literacy instruction in terms of a whole-part-whole framework. She advocated beginning with a whole text, then focusing on specific parts of the text using planned skills instruction, and then returning to the text for application and practice. The goal of a balanced literacy program is to develop independent readers and writers by balancing direct skills instruction with authentic reading and writing.

☐ THE ROLE OF PHONICS INSTRUCTION: RECENT DEVELOPMENTS

To help bring resolution to the increasingly bitter battle between advocates of whole language and those of phonics instruction, the International Reading Association (IRA, 1997) issued a position paper asserting, "The teaching of phonics is an important aspect of beginning reading," but cautioned that effective phonics instruction "must be embedded in the context of a total reading/language arts program" (p. 2).

The IRA statement was one indication of widespread support for phonics instruction. A survey of elementary teachers by Baumann, Hoffman, Moon, and Duffy-Hester (1998) was another indication. That study found that 98% of elementary teachers believed phonics skills were essential to the teaching of reading.

THE NATIONAL READING PANEL REPORT

In 2000, the National Institute for Literacy issued the report of the National Reading Panel (NRP) on teaching children to read. The report was intended to examine scientific research published since 1970 on reading instruction and to make conclusions.

Not surprisingly, the section of the NRP report that dealt with phonics was the most controversial. Because the panel accepted only formal experimental studies with control groups, conclusions were based on only 38 research studies with a total of 66 comparison groups. The panel concluded that phonics instruction does "make a significant contribution to children's growth in reading" (p. 2-132). The panel also stated:

Phonics instruction is most effective when it begins early, in kindergarten or 1st grade.

Phonics is effective in helping to prevent reading difficulties and to remediate disabled readers, but not necessarily with older, low-achieving students.

Phonics instruction improved the reading comprehension and spelling of younger children and disabled readers, but had mixed results for older students.

Children of all socio-economic levels benefited from phonics instruction.

Interestingly, the panel was not able to conclude whether one type of phonics instruction was more effective than another.

The NRP's report came under attack as "fatally flawed" (Garan, 2001) with errors in validity, reliability, and generalizability. It was specifically criticized for inflating the importance of phonics to reading instruction. Krashen (2001) warned against interpreting the NRP's results as an endorsement of skill-based methods at the expense of methods that emphasize comprehension. Ehri and Stahl (2001), two authors of the report, countered these charges with this statement: "The NRP report reiterates what many teachers recognize: phonics instruction is one ingredient of a successful reading program. Why such a clear and obvious finding is so threatening to some people remains a puzzle" (p. 20).

NO CHILD LEFT BEHIND AND STATE STANDARDS

The NRP's report on reading failed to end the reading wars, but its emphasis on scientifically based research had a profound impact on new legislation that would change the way schools operated across the country. In 2001, President Bush introduced the No Child Left Behind (NCLB) Act, designed to increase accountability, provide more flexibility for parents, and emphasize reading instruction (U.S. Department of Education, 2003).

The reading initiative portion of the NCLB Act, called "Reading First," provided grants only for those reading programs that were "informed by scientifically based reading research" (U.S. Department of Education, 2003). Grant proposals also had to ensure that students were "systematically and explicitly taught" five reading skills: phonemic awareness, phonics, fluency, vocabulary, and comprehension.

The NCLB Act also required that students in grades 3 through 8 be tested annually based on "challenging state standards in reading and mathematics." As a result, states designed reading standards for all grade levels, often based on findings of the NRP, which became the basis of proficiency tests (also called high-stakes tests, because passing them is often a requirement for graduation).

Standards are explicit statements that identify what all students on a particular grade level should know and be able to do. **Standards-based education** is a system for using these standards in order to develop curriculum and assessment. The language arts standards for the state of Ohio (Ohio Department of Education [ODE], 2001) are, perhaps, typical of state standards. One of the 10 standards is "[p]honemic awareness, word recognition and fluency." Each standard is accompanied by benchmarks that specify goals students are expected to achieve after a certain number of years in school. For example, the phonemic awareness standard has a benchmark stating that students at the end of the grades K through 3 program should be able to "[u]se letter-sound correspondence knowledge and structural analysis to decode words" (ODE, 2001, p. 181).

In addition to the benchmarks, the Ohio standards include specific objectives (grade-level indicators) for each grade level. For example, one indicator for grade 1 states that students should be able to "[a]dd, delete or change sounds in a given word to create new or rhyming words" (ODE, 2001, p. 181).

☐ ASSESSING PHONICS

Today's standards-based education demands that students be regularly assessed for comprehension. Although formal tests of phonics are available, assessment should be an integral part of instruction and linked to the students' reading in class rather than from an outside test that is devoid of context. Each chapter of this book provides informal assessments that are easy to give and interpret. These assessments can be used by teachers to help their students become better readers.

☐ PHONICS IN A COMPREHENSIVE LANGUAGE ARTS PROGRAM

Research makes it clear that phonics is an important part of reading instruction. In addition, state standards and mandates from the No Child Left Behind legislation require that phonics be explicitly taught to students. However, this should not be interpreted to mean that phonics is all that should be taught or that it should be taught as a separate subject. Instruction in phonics and word identification should be incorporated in the kind of comprehensive language arts program that is suggested by the IRA/NCTE Standards for the English Language Arts (1996). Such a comprehensive program would include:

Reflections on the purposes, forms, and structures of language

Instruction that includes oral and written language

Teacher modeling of a wide range of strategies for interpreting and creating texts

Guidance to help students use strategies with increasing independence

Opportunities for students to make discoveries about the forms and structures of language through extensive reading and writing

Careful monitoring of students' progress to better plan instruction

Exploration of meaningful ideas and human relationships through language

This book helps to highlight principles and practices that support development in word identification and phonics within the larger contexts of literacy and language.

☐ ☐ ☐ ☐ ☐

🔳 BEFORE YOU MOVE ON

Check Your Understanding
Before you move on, reflect on your learning by rating your understanding of the following key terms and concepts.

Mark + next to those items you understand and can explain.

Mark − next to those items you are beginning to understand, but that are still not clear.

Mark ? next to those items that seem unfamiliar or confusing.

_____ Meaning emphasis versus code emphasis

_____ Segmenting and blending

_____ Whole language

_____ National Reading Panel

_____ No Child Left Behind

_____ Academic content standards

_____ Standards-based education

_____ Balanced literacy approach

_____ Whole-part-whole instructional framework

Be sure to return to this list as you continue reading the text to see how your understanding of these issues has grown.

WHAT'S IN THIS CHAPTER FOR ME?

Early Childhood Teachers

No doubt the most important job you will have as a teacher in the primary grades will be to teach your students how to read and write. Phonics and word identification is an essential component of this responsibility. If you reread the results of research on phonics instruction, you will see that phonics instruction is most effective when begun early (NRP report). Even if you teach preschool or kindergarten students, you will be teaching many phonics skills. Be sure to check out your state standards by following the directions in Figure 1.1. These

■ **FIGURE 1.1   What Are Your State's Standards?**

Take the following steps to find out what standards your state uses to teach reading.

1. Go to your state's department of education homepage or do a keyword search using "Name of State standards" and select the state department of education homepage.

2. Click on reading/language arts standards and read them. Your state considers these to be the most important elements involved in teaching reading. How much emphasis is put on phonics and word identification?

3. Look at the objectives for a grade level you would like to teach. What are the phonics/word identification objectives for this grade level?

4. Compare these objectives to the conclusions of the National Reading Panel. For a more detailed comparison, visit the NRP website at *www.nationalreadingpanel.org*

■ FIGURE 1.2   Planning a Lesson for Primary Grade Students Based
                on State Standards

Standard: Phonemic Awareness, Word Recognition, and Fluency

First Grade Level Indicator: "Add, delete or change sounds in a given word to create new or rhyming words" (ODE, 2001)

Materials: *Jack and Jill* poem; prepared letter cards: b, ch, f, d, k, m, p, sp, st, w

Procedure

1. Read the poem *Jack and Jill* to students. Ask students to identify the word with the same ending sound as *Jill* and write *Jill* and *hill* on the chalkboard.

2. Have students circle the part of each word that is the same. Explain that words with the same ending sound (not necessarily the same spelling) rhyme, and that we can make more rhyming words by changing the beginning sound.

3. Write only *-ill* on the board. Without looking, have students choose a letter card from a box, and write that letter in front of *-ill*. Have the student and the rest of the class say the new word created. Continue with the other letters.

Assessment

1. Erase the board and have students write five real words with the *-ill* chunk. (You could also add any other previously learned chunks, such as *-at*.)

2. As they finish, have students bring their papers to you and read each word to you aloud.

3. Check off the words read correctly and use the following criteria for evaluation

    Five words written and read correctly = understanding

    Three or four words written and read correctly = may need additional help

    Less than three words written and read correctly = needs reteaching

---

are the objectives you will use in your teaching, so please familiarize yourself with them. Figure 1.2 provides a step-by-step model of how to use standards to plan lessons in phonics and word identification that are appropriate and interesting to young children. Be sure to read carefully the section on defining phonics and how phonics should not be viewed as a separate subject taught with workbook pages, but part of an overall language arts program. You will learn more about this approach in the upcoming chapters.

Middle Grade Teachers

You may be wondering what phonics and this book have to do with you. After all, older students presumably know how to read. This is a dangerous assumption. Some of your students will not be proficient readers and will need your help in decoding words.

You may view yourself as essentially a teacher of a content area such as science, math, or social studies. These areas include many new and difficult

■ FIGURE 1.3   Planning a Lesson for Middle Grade Students Based
on State Standards

Standard: Acquisition of Vocabulary

Sixth Grade Level Indicator: "Apply the knowledge of prefixes, suffixes, and roots and their various inflections to analyze the meanings of words" (ODE, 2001)

Specific Objective: To introduce students to the meaning of four of the most common prefixes: *re-, un-, dis-,* and *pre-*

Materials: Overhead of nine words with the prefix *re-*, and the word *reptile*. Handouts for each group of students with 30 words with prefixes and four "ringer words"

Procedure

1. Display the overhead of words with *re-* prefixes. Ask students what the words have in common. Use the words *prefix* and *root word* to demonstrate the two parts of the words.

2. Have students go through the list and explain how the prefix influences the meaning of the word, for example, *review* means to look at something again.

3. Have the students find the "ringer word" in which *re* is not acting as a prefix (*reptile*) and cross it out.

4. Now have students work in groups. Give them a list of 30 words with *un, dis,* and *pre* at the beginning. Have them write the words in groups according to the prefix. After reading all of the words, students should write the meaning of the prefix and cross out any words in which the beginning is not a prefix.

Group Assessment

Have each group share their findings and assess their answers according to the following criteria

All of the words are sorted correctly under each prefix

Each prefix has a correct definition, for example, *un* means "not"

Each group is able to find the ringer words that do not fit the prefix rule

Individual Assessment

Give each student a mixed list of words using the four prefixes. Have students write a definition of each word using the prefix.

---

words that your students will need your help in understanding. Phonics is one strategy that will help them to unlock those words.

The ability of your students to understand content areas and to pass proficiency tests on these subjects is completely dependent on their ability to read effectively. Be sure to check out your state standards by following the directions in Figure 1.1. Word identification objectives for middle grades may be listed under *Vocabulary* standards. Figure 1.3 provides a step-by-step example of how to use standards to plan lessons in word identification that are appropriate and motivating for older students.

Intervention Specialists

As an intervention specialist you will be dealing with many students who have problems with reading. See the section on "Intervention When Students Struggle" for ideas about your role in helping below-level readers. If you reread the findings of the National Reading Panel, you will see that phonics has been found to be effective in helping to prevent reading difficulties and to remediate disabled readers. Do not assume, however, that students with reading problems need to be constantly drilled with phonics rules or given endless worksheets to complete. Teach phonics as one helpful strategy to unlock words among other ones, which you will learn about in the coming chapters.

In addition to looking at the research on phonics, be sure to check state standards by following the directions in Figure 1.1. Look at a variety of grade levels to see expectations for student achievement. Keep in mind that the vast majority of your students will be expected to pass the same grade-level proficiency tests as their peers. Finally read Figures 1.2 and 1.3 for models of how to create interesting lessons for students using state standards.

MAKING DECISIONS ABOUT INSTRUCTION: WHAT TEACHERS NEED TO KNOW

I magine two first-grade classrooms that are adjacent to each other. In classroom 1, teacher A holds up a large card with the letter *a* written on it. She asks the students to make the short /a/ sound, and they all enthusiastically respond by saying, "A-a-ah, a-a-ah, apple." She does the same with the letters *h* and *t*. After putting the three letter cards on a tray, teacher A asks the children to watch carefully as she "pushes the sounds together" to say the word *hat*.

The children practice blending other letters to say the words *man, sad,* and *cab.* Teacher A then directs the children to take out their workbooks and turn to page 6. They are to circle all the pictures on the page that have a short *a* vowel and then color them neatly.

Next door in classroom 2, teacher Z reads the last page of *The Gingerbread Man* (Kimmel, 1993). The students enthusiastically join in the refrain, "Run, run as fast as you can. You can't catch me, I'm the Gingerbread Man!" Teacher Z then takes transparent yellow tape and highlights the words *can* and *man.* He asks the children what "chunk" is the same in each word. The children easily recognize the -*an* chunk. Teacher Z then writes the word *than* on the board. He asks, "If you did not know this word, how could the other words help you?" The children respond that *can* and *man* rhyme with *than* and all you have to do is change the beginning chunk to the /th/ sound.

Teacher Z directs the students to work in small groups to write as many *-an* words as possible. He then tells them to circle the word that they think should go on the class's "word" wall to represent the *-an* chunk. Eventually, the whole class votes on the final choice: "man."

Before you read the rest of this chapter, consider these questions:

- What similarities do you see between the two lessons?
- What differences do you notice?
- Which lesson do you think would be more effective? Why?

As you continue to read this chapter, see how your initial impressions of these two lessons parallel research findings and expert opinion.

APPROACHES TO PHONICS INSTRUCTION

Chapter 1 showed that research supports the importance of instruction in sounds and symbols but has not identified a single method for teaching phonics as the best. This suggests that teachers need to know a variety of instructional techniques and be prepared to choose those that are most appropriate for their students. In this chapter, we present a brief overview of major approaches to instruction and state principles that can guide the decisions that teachers need to make when planning instruction.

Consider the scenario that opened this chapter. Teacher A and Teacher Z were both concerned with helping their students to learn about letters and sounds, but their lessons showed significant differences in their focus, materials, and the roles taken by teacher and students. Stahl, Duffy-Hester, and Stahl (1998) identified five systematic approaches to teaching phonics: synthetic and analytic phonics, which are considered traditional approaches, and spelling-based, analogy, and embedded phonics, which are contemporary phonics approaches. Each of these approaches is represented to some extent in the lessons in the scenario.

TRADITIONAL APPROACHES

Teacher A uses two traditional approaches to phonics instruction. When she asks her students to sound out (or segment) individual letter sounds and then blend those sounds into words, she is using a **synthetic phonics** approach, one in which students "build" a word from its component sounds. This method can be effective for decoding words that are phonetically regular, but has its limitations when applied to a word in which a letter does not make its typical sound (such as the *u* in *bush*) or a word with a silent letter (such as *comb*).

The National Reading Panel (2000) identified two difficulties with synthetic phonics. First, when articulating the individual sounds, children will often add an extra sound, just as the students in teacher A's room added an *h* when they said "aah" for the short /a/ sound. The second problem is that when students attempt to blend the sounds, especially when the word has more than three sounds, it is hard for them to remember and say the sounds in the correct order.

Teacher A also used an **analytical approach** to phonics when she asked students to identify other words with the short /a/ sound. In this method, students are asked to "break down" a known word into its component sounds. For example, students who can identify the word *red* might be guided to see that the same short /e/ sound occurs in *bet* and the same /r/ sound occurs in *rat*.

Traditional approaches to phonics instruction often involve using special materials such as workbooks or texts that contain only phonetically regular words or other common words that students can read using their existing knowledge of phonics. Some critics contend that these materials do not prepare students to read "real" books. Patricia Cunningham, who has written extensively about phonics instruction, expressed concern that the emphasis that traditional approaches place on the sound made by each letter will give students the wrong idea about reading so that, "they will get in the habit of 'sounding out' every word—and that is not how good readers read" (Cunningham, 2000, p. 183).

CONTEMPORARY APPROACHES

Teacher Z uses several approaches to phonics that Stahl et al. (1998) called "contemporary." First, he teaches phonics skills within the context of real literature. This is called an **embedded approach** to phonics. In Chapter 5, you will see many other examples of how to use this approach. Teacher Z also uses an *analogy approach* called **decoding by analogy** or **compare/contrast.** Using this method, students learn to compare a known word with new ones, but rather than looking at individual letters, they look for familiar patterns of letters which they call "chunks."

Most words can be divided into two or more chunks. For example, the word *thank* has a beginning chunk *th*, which is technically called an **onset.** An onset consists of all the consonants before a vowel in a syllable. The ending chunk -*ank* is called the **rime,** which contains the vowel and the rest of the syllable. Students using an analogy method understand that if they know the word *thank*, then they can figure out other words such as *plank*, and they can possibly use their knowledge of the *-ank* chunk to read longer words such as *Frankenstein.*

Researchers such as Goswami (2000) have found that rime chunks are more consistent in their pronunciation than individual letters and are therefore easier for students to remember and use. In a recent study (White, 2005), second-grade students in classes where the teachers were trained to use an analogy-based approach to phonics performed better on tests of word identification and reading comprehension than students in classes that used more traditional approaches to phonics. Critics of this approach point out, however, that sooner or later every reader needs to learn the sounds represented by individual letters.

Teacher Z's lesson also included a **spelling approach** to teaching phonics. He combined spelling instruction with phonics by asking students to write words with a particular rime pattern. Many educational researchers (Bear, Invernizzi, Templeton, & Johnson, 2000; Pinnell & Fountas, 1998) have found that phonics instruction is most effective when writing goes hand in hand with reading. Knowing and using common letter patterns to spell words correctly is called **orthographic knowledge.** A list of the most common rime patterns that could be used to teach both spelling and word identification is found in Chapter 4.

Notice that the contemporary approaches used by teacher Z use only children's literature and blank paper, rather than workbooks or other prepared materials. Students are also given a bit more control of the lesson. Instead of giving students a list of words with the *-an* chunk to read, teacher Z asked the students to generate their own lists, and he gave them a choice of which word would go on the class word wall to represent that chunk.

Advocates of contemporary approaches believe that students who can make such choices will learn more because they are more actively involved in their own learning. On the other hand, the National Reading Panel report (2000) concluded that the most effective reading programs were the ones that were direct and systematic in their instruction, and some critics argue that contemporary approaches may be a little less systematic because the teacher does not entirely control the activities.

We agree with Tompkins (2006) that "the best way to teach phonics is through a combination of direct instruction and application activities" (p. 130). Although we tend to favor a contemporary approach to teaching phonics, we recognize that teachers must be free to make instructional decisions that match their own beliefs, the overall literacy program, and the specific needs of their students. We also believe that there are general principles that should guide instruction regardless of the particular methods teachers employ. Those principles are based on research into the process of reading and the development of readers, on years of classroom practice, and on our own beliefs about the nature of literacy and learning.

☐ PRINCIPLE 1: TEACHERS MUST SHOW STUDENTS HOW TO USE CUES TO IDENTIFY WORDS

As discussed in Chapter 1, phonics is best understood as part of the larger issue of how readers make sense from text. All teachers of reading must have a basic understanding of the almost magical process by which black marks on a white page are transformed into words and ideas. The key to this understanding is the notion that readers are involved in an active process of piecing together meaning from a variety of information sources. These information sources are generally called **cues** or **cueing systems.** The terms that are used to label cueing systems may seem a little confusing or complicated at first. To understand them, begin by remembering that some of the cues that readers use to create meaning are on the page, and some are in the reader's head.

GRAPHOPHONEMIC CUES

The system most concerned with cues that are on the page is the **graphophonemic cueing system,** a term that literally means "writing sounds." To become more aware of how you use this system, consider the following sentence:

> **Heather gasped in horror as she looked at her zarp hairdo in the mirror.**

You can pronounce the word *zarp* by looking at the letters that are part of it and using the information you have about the sounds that letters make. You know the sound that *z* makes, and you know other words that have the *-arp* spelling pattern, such as *harp* and *sharp*. You use this knowledge when decoding this word.

The smallest unit of sound in a language is called a **phoneme.** When we refer to the sound or phoneme of a letter or letters, it is written like /t/. **Graphemes** are the written representation of phoneme sounds. These are usually single letters, but they can be more than one letter, such as *th*, because *th* represents only one sound as in *think*. Similarly, not all letters are graphemes because some letters in a word may not represent a sound. In the word *bake*, the *e* is a letter but not a phoneme because it is silent and does not make a sound.

English would be a much easier language if there were a one-to-one correspondence between letters and sounds. Unfortunately, this is not the case. There are 26 letters in the English language, but 44 sounds (phonemes) because letters can represent more than one sound. For example the letter *a* sounds different in *cat, about, cave, draw, car,* and *call*. To make things even more complicated, phonemes can be represented by different graphemes. The long /a/ sound can be written as *maid, stay, they, weigh,* or *late*.

Proficient readers of English know these facts about their language, even if they are not always aware of that knowledge. They use those understandings when they try to figure out words. Helping students to build and use their knowledge about graphemes and phonemes when they read and write is a large part of teaching them to read.

USING MEANING CUES: THE SEMANTIC AND SYNTACTIC SYSTEMS

Knowledge about letters and sounds is important, but identifying the word *zarp* requires other knowledge as well. Once you figured out the likely sound of the word, you probably did a quick mental inventory to check whether you know a word that fits those sounds. Finding no such word, you may then have considered the meanings of the other words in the sentence to conclude that *zarp* must mean "awful or ugly." The words *gasped* and *horror* might suggest some kind of horrible accident, but your background knowledge tells you that these words could also apply to a girl having a very bad hair day.

When you consider the possible meaning of a word or try to identify it by using the meaning of a sentence or passage and your own background knowledge, you are using the **semantic cueing system.** In short, semantic cues are those that have to do with "sense" rather than the "sound" of words.

The third cueing system is the **syntactic cueing system.** Just as the graphophonemic system consists of patterns or "rules" about how letters are connected to sounds, the syntactic system consists of patterns or rules about the ways in which words can and cannot be put together in sentences. In other words, it is the "grammar" of a particular language. You might have confirmed your conclusion about the probable meaning of *zarp* through your understanding that its position in front of the word *hairdo* signals that it is describing that word. As an English speaker, you have that understanding even if you cannot use the proper labels to say that it is an adjective modifying a noun.

If the sentence had read, "Heather zarped when she looked at her hairdo," then you would conclude that *zarped* was a verb because of its position after the noun, but also because of the additional clue of the suffix -*ed* added to the word. Children do not need to know the names of the parts of speech to use syntactical cues. They have been hearing common sentence patterns since they were born and can use that experience as they constuct meaning with written language.

HOW READERS COMBINE CUES

Cueing systems can be discussed separately, but readers probably never use just one kind of cue independently. They may, however, focus on some cues more consciously than others. In the *zarp* example, for instance, you may have used the syntactic system fairly unconsciously to confirm that your conclusion about the probable meaning of the word fit with the way the sentence was arranged. Good readers generally shift their attention from "sound" cues to "sense" cues and back again easily and fairly unconsciously. If they cannot do so, they may struggle. Goodman's (1985) research on cueing systems indicated that some readers tend to overuse graphophonemic cues. They attempt to sound out every word without regard to the meaning or structure of the sentence.

For students to learn to use and balance the three cueing systems, they need experiences in which they are faced with unknown words in a context that provides useful syntactic and semantic cues. Contemporary approaches to instruction may be particularly well suited for this purpose because they use natural literature. Worksheets and books with carefully controlled vocabulary are, in a sense, designed so that students will not *need* to use meaning cues. Teachers who use traditional instructional approaches must be deliberate about modeling the process of identifying unknown words by combining cues and creating opportunities for students to practice.

All teachers can help students learn to integrate cues by encouraging them to attempt rather than skip unknown words and to try to "figure out" rather than "sound out" those words. Students can learn to monitor their own attempts by asking themselves the following three questions.

1. Does _____ make sense in the sentence? (semantic cueing)
2. Does the sentence sound like a real sentence? (syntactic cueing)
3. Does _____ match the letters of the word and their sounds? (graphophonemic cueing)

In the middle grades, students can be asked to reflect on their word identification process and then to explain it, either orally or in writing. The class might, for example, collaborate to create a bulletin board listing the "Top Ten Ways to Figure Out a Difficult Word."

☐ PRINCIPLE 2: TEACHERS MUST EXTEND THE ALPHABETIC KNOWLEDGE AND PHONEMIC AWARENESS THAT CHILDREN DEVELOP AT HOME

LETTER AND ALPHABETIC KNOWLEDGE

Understandings about phonics and word identification usually begin long before children come to school. Even very young children often develop **letter knowledge,** the ability to identify letters of the alphabet. Parents may believe that their child has letter knowledge because he or she can recite the ABC song, but true letter knowledge involves being able to identify letters in isolation and to distinguish uppercase and lowercase forms of letters. For example, when George points to the first letter of his name and says, "That's a *g*," he is demonstrating letter knowledge.

When children grasp the concept that their parents are producing bedtime stories from the mysterious squiggles on the page rather than from their own imaginations, they are on the way to developing **alphabetic knowledge,** the understanding that letters represent sounds and that speech can be written down.

Teachers must be prepared to build on whatever knowledge about letters and sounds that children bring to the classroom. They can, for instance, demonstrate the alphabetic principle by transcribing their students' oral language on chart paper. They can also surround students with print and frequently invite them to name uppercase and lowercase letters. Finally, teachers must create an environment in which students who have had the literacy experiences that lead to letter and alphabetic knowledge can naturally share what they know with students who have not yet developed that knowledge.

PHONEMIC AWARENESS

The ability to use the graphophonemic system requires both an understanding of written symbols (letter and alphabetic knowledge) and the ability to distinguish and manipulate phonemes in spoken words, which is called **phonemic awareness.** A child who can segment individual sounds in the word *dog*, count how many there are, and say those sounds individually is showing evidence of phonemic awareness. A child who can listen to the sounds /f/ /a/ /s/ /t/ and blend them to say the word *fast* is also showing evidence of phonemic awareness.

Readers with strong phonemic awareness can listen to the words *hill, Jill,* and *hit* and easily tell that *hill* and *Jill* rhyme and that *hit* begins with the same sound as *hill* but not the same as *Jill*. Readers can also say that the word *car* is left when you take off the /t/ sound from *cart*.

A great deal of attention has been focused on phonemic awareness in recent years. Research has found that it has a tremendous influence on beginning to read (reading acquisition). Share, Jorm, Maclean, and Matthews (1984) found phonemic awareness to be the number one predictor of success in reading, better than such variables as socioeconomic status, gender, preschool attendance, or even the amount of time the child was read to at home. Some experts now believe that lack of phonemic awareness may be the root cause of many reading disabilities including dyslexia (Fawcett & Nicolson, 1995).

The good news is that 80% of children will develop phonemic awareness by mid first grade. The bad news is that the remaining 20% are at risk of never becoming proficient readers. The National Reading Panel (2000) reviewed 52 studies on phonemic awareness and came to the following conclusions:

- Phonemic awareness can be taught.
- Phonemic awareness assists children to learn to read.
- Phonemic awareness instruction helped all types of students including struggling readers, preschoolers, kindergartners, first graders, children in grades 2 through 6 (most of whom were struggling readers), children in all socioeconomic status (SES) levels, and English language learners.
- Phonemic awareness should not be considered a complete reading program and is most effective when combined with phonics instruction.

The International Reading Association (IRA, 1998) issued a position statement that acknowledged the importance of phonemic awareness, but cautioned against practices such as drilling students on phonemes for specific amounts of time each day. We agree with the IRA's position that "interaction with print combined with explicit attention to sound structure in words is the best vehicle toward growth."

Like alphabetic knowledge, phonemic awareness may be developed at home as children listen to storybooks, particularly those that feature rhyming or other highly patterned language. Teachers can build on that foundation and develop phonemic awareness in a natural way within a meaningful context. The following plan is one example:

1. Select literature that plays with the sounds in language and emphasizes rhythm, rhyme, and alliteration. Suggestions include:
   - Nursery rhymes or simple poems
   - Dr. Seuss books: *Fox in Socks* (1965), *Hop on Pop* (1963), *Green Eggs and Ham* (1988)
   - Bill Martin books: *Brown Bear, Brown Bear What Do You See?* (1967), *Chicka Chicka Boom Boom* (1989)
   - Nancy Shaw books: *Sheep in a Jeep* (1986), *Sheep on a Ship* (1986)
2. During rereadings of the text, play language games that emphasize phonemic awareness and involve all students.
   - Choral read a phrase with two rhyming words, then fade out your voice and let the students supply the missing rhyming word.
   - Ask students to listen for words that begin (or end) with the same sound.
   - Choose a multisyllable word from the text and ask students to clap the number of beats in the word.
   - Ask students to segment a word into phonemes by "stretching it out" so they can hear each sound.
   - Say the sounds of a word and ask students to say the whole word.

■ FIGURE 2.1   Sound Boxes

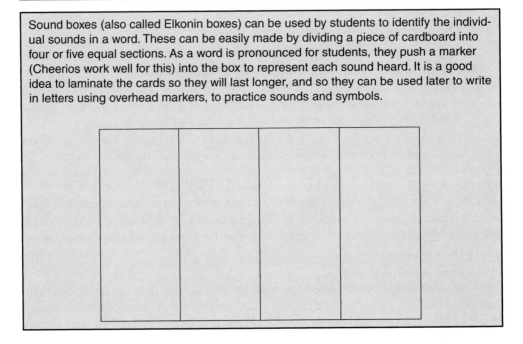

Sound boxes (also called Elkonin boxes) can be used by students to identify the individual sounds in a word. These can be easily made by dividing a piece of cardboard into four or five equal sections. As a word is pronounced for students, they push a marker (Cheerios work well for this) into the box to represent each sound heard. It is a good idea to laminate the cards so they will last longer, and so they can be used later to write in letters using overhead markers, to practice sounds and symbols.

■ Select a word from the text and ask students to figure out how it would sound if you changed part of it; For example, "What would *run* sound like if it started with a /f/ sound?"

Figure 2.1 describes an activity called sound boxes, which is useful for helping young children segment sounds they hear in words.

☐ PRINCIPLE 3: TEACHING WORD IDENTIFICATION IS BASED ON AN UNDERSTANDING OF DEVELOPMENT

Letter knowledge, alphabetic knowledge, and phonemic awareness are three important milestones that generally develop early in a student's reading development. To guide students' progress in identifying words, teachers need a more complete picture of what students need to learn and when they can be expected to learn it. Ehri (1998) identified five developmental stages of word identification: prealphabetic, partial alphabetic, alphabetic, consolidated, and automatic. By being aware of these stages, teachers can more easily recognize what strategies a student is already using and which ones that student may be ready to learn.

PREALPHABETIC STAGE

Children at the prealphabetic stage, usually from preschool to kindergarten, lack alphabetic knowledge. They do not associate letters with sounds and may not know the concept of a word. They can often, however, recognize some words because of their unique logos and color, such as a McDonald's sign or a stop sign. Having knowledge of such **environmental print,** and identifying it, is considered a legitimate first step toward literacy. When they are asked to write, children in this phase will often scribble or draw a picture. They may be able to write some letters, such as the letters in their name, but they will not associate the letters with a particular sound. Teachers can help students at this stage by:

- Showing them where words begin and end and pointing to each word while reading together
- Doing phonemic awareness activities
- Helping them use the pictures in a book to infer meaning
- Helping them to associate letters with sounds (Using the letters in their names and their classmates' names is a good place to start.)

PARTIAL ALPHABETIC STAGE

In the partial alphabetic stage, children (usually from kindergarten to beginning first grade) know most of the letter names and the sounds of most consonants, along with some vowel sounds, usually the short ones. The children use this knowledge in their writing and begin to use one or more consonant letters to represent a word, for example, *dg* for *dog.* Teachers can help students at this stage by:

- Encouraging them to look for letters, particularly first letters, as cues that can be used to figure out words
- Encouraging them to write by using **invented (phonetic) spelling** of words.

At this stage of development, students will learn more about letters and sounds by attempting to figure out the correct spelling than they will by looking it up or having the teacher supply it immediately.

ALPHABETIC STAGE

In late kindergarten or early first grade, students usually begin to pay more attention to vowel sounds. They are ready to analyze all the letters in a word in order to decode it. When they spell a word, students in the alphabetic stage will write a letter for each sound they hear, but because of the irregular nature

Invented Spelling in Environmental Print.

of English spelling, they may not produce the conventional spelling, for example, *red* for *read*. Teachers can help students in this phase by:

■ Encouraging students to look for familiar rime chunks in words and use the compare/contrast method

■ Encouraging students to use all three cueing systems when reading

■ Insisting that students try to self-correct errors

■ Insisting that students spell selected high-frequency words correctly

■ Encouraging students to use rime chunks to spell words

CONSOLIDATED STAGE

By the end of second grade to the beginning of fourth grade, most children enter the consolidated stage. Children are experienced in reading and writing chunks of words and expand their strategies to include prefixes, suffixes, and other affixes. Students can now focus more on comprehension than decoding and may only need to stop and analyze words that are proper names or words outside their speaking vocabulary. Teachers working with these students should:

■ Teach strategies for analyzing multisyllable words

■ Encourage independence in word identification and comprehension

■ Work toward conventional spelling

AUTOMATIC STAGE

At the automatic stage, students can instantly recognize most of the words they encounter in print and can focus on their most important job, comprehending the text. Students are able to apply their own strategies and learn new words by using resources other than the teacher. Spelling often lags behind reading, but students at this stage can spell most common words correctly. Reading is characterized by fluency and independence.

Many students in the middle grades are just entering the automatic stage. Teachers at this level may be surprised at the spelling errors students make and suspect that "laziness" is the cause. This suspicion is caused by the mistaken assumption that students who "know phonics" well enough to read fluently will also be able to spell correctly.

Notice that the lessons in the opening scenario fit the developmental characteristics that are typically found in first grade. They contain elements that address the needs of students at both the partial alphabetic and the alphabetic stage. Even in the first grade, children will not always be at the same developmental stage, and the range of differences can be expected to grow wider as they progress through school.

☐ PRINCIPLE 4: TEACHERS MUST KNOW APPROPRIATE INTERVENTIONS FOR STUDENTS WHO STRUGGLE

Although differences in the rate of development are natural and unavoidable, some students may struggle to make progress either temporarily or long term. The causes for these difficulties can be complex, but teachers need to be prepared to make adjustments in their instruction that will support the growth of all students.

Some difficulties in learning phonics and word identification are the result of specific learning disabilities. Children with learning disabilities have a significant discrepancy between their cognitive abilities and their actual performance. In other words, they do not perform as well in academic tasks as one would expect. For example, a child in fourth grade who scores in the normal range on an intelligence test but is reading at an early primary level may have a specific learning disability in written language.

Dyslexia is the name used for a severe form of learning disability in reading. In the past, dyslexia was often characterized as "word blindness," a condition in which students reversed letters and had trouble focusing on print. Recent brain scan technology has revealed, however, that dyslexia may be better described as "sound blindness." Shaywitz (2003) reported that people with dyslexia find it extremely difficult to hear and manipulate phonemes, and this lack of phonemic awareness is the root cause of their reading disabilities.

■ FIGURE 2.2   Phonemic Awareness and the Older, Struggling Reader

Several studies (Bradley & Bryant, 1983; Bruck, 1992; Fawcett & Nicolson, 1995) have found evidence for a causal link between poor phonemic awareness and severe reading problems especially in older students. The National Reading Panel (2000) examined several programs that emphasized phonemic awareness for older, at-risk readers and found that they significantly improved their ability to read words, but not necessarily to spell them.

Older students need age-appropriate materials that will motivate, not embarrass, them. We suggest using alternative texts such as popular song lyrics, contemporary poetry and rap, tongue twisters, and even commercial jingles to emphasize the sounds in language. Following are examples:

Alliteration: Find phrases in popular magazines or song lyrics that have the same beginning sounds, "That girl got game." Dictate or write tongue twisters and challenge other students to read them as quickly as possible.

Assonance: Listen for and identify the same medial sounds in words such as *baby, date, today, crave.*

Rhyming: Locate rhyming words in your favorite song. Create a rhyming dictionary to record these. Discuss the different spellings of rhyming words (e.g., *blue, you, do, few, through, too*). Choose a product to sell. Dictate or write a rhyming jingle that will stick in the public's head and sell your product.

Figure 2.2 describes how phonemic awareness impacts older students who have problems with reading.

INTERVENTION WHEN STUDENTS STRUGGLE

Direct teaching of letters, sounds, and word patterns has been found to be effective when teaching students with learning disabilities. Gaskins (1998a) founded the Benchmark School for students with severe reading difficulties. She created a reading program based on an analogy approach to phonics in which students are taught 120 key words that are displayed on a word wall like a dictionary, just as Mr. Z did in his classroom. Students learn to compare and contrast those words with new words that they encounter when reading.

The process of meeting the needs of all students can be compared to coaching athletes. A coach demonstrates techniques for playing the game successfully and guides the players as they practice them. The coach also works with individuals to help them build on their strengths and work on areas that need improvement. Ultimately, though, players must play the game on their own.

Coaching reading is a similar process. The teacher demonstrates skills and strategies that all students will need when they are reading, often through short **mini lessons** that can be applied immediately to actual reading. Teachers also do individual coaching with students, often in a small group or one-on-one setting as they engage in guided practice. The ultimate goal is to produce confident, independent readers. As Vacca, Vacca, Gove, Burkey, Lenhart, and Mckeon (2003) note, "The teacher who coaches prepares, models, guides, supports, and stretches students to the limits of their potential as readers and writers" (p. 43).

☐ PRINCIPLE 5: TEACHERS MUST GUIDE THEIR INSTRUCTION ABOUT PHONICS AND WORD IDENTIFICATION THROUGH ONGOING ASSESSMENT

The International Reading Association has identified the ability to use assessment tools effectively as one of its five standards for reading professionals. The standard states that classroom teachers should be able to "analyze, compare, contrast, and use assessment results to plan, evaluate, and revise effective instruction for all students within an assessment/evaluation/ instruction cycle" (p. 15).

ASSESSING PHONEMIC AWARENESS

You can see some of the ways in which a teacher might use assessment to guide instruction by considering the role of assessment in teaching phonemic awareness. By careful observation in the classroom, a teacher might identify students who are having difficulty hearing rhyming words in class poems. Then the teacher could use an informal written assessment such as the one shown in Figure 2.3. Based on the results, the teacher could plan instruction for those readers.

▨ BEFORE YOU MOVE ON

Check Your Understanding
Examine each of the following pairs and try to explain how the term on the left differs from that on the right.

Synthetic phonics	versus	analytic phonics
Embedded instruction	versus	traditional approach
Decoding by analogy	versus	spelling-based approach
Alphabetic knowledge	versus	letter knowledge
Semantic cues	versus	graphophonemic cues

A.   Rhyming

Ask: Do these words rhyme? Tell me yes or no.

Child's Response   Scoring (+) = correct, (−) = incorrect, (?) = did not give
answer

1.   dog   log   _____   _____

2.   bat   boat   _____   _____

3.   berry   cherry   _____   _____

Total: 3/3 = understands   2/3 = unsure   0–1 = does not know

B.   Beginning Sounds

Say: Do these words start with the same sound? Tell me yes or no.

1.   red   nut   _____   _____

2.   cheese   checkers   _____   _____

3.   like   lunch   _____   _____

Total: 3/3 = understands   2/3 = unsure   0–1 = does not know

C.   Sound Blending

Say: I am going to say the sounds in a word very slowly. See if you can guess my word.
Practice /m/ /e/

1.   /g/ /o/   _____   _____

2.   /l/ /i/ /p/   _____   _____

3.   /sh/ /ee/ /p/   _____   _____

Total: 3/3 = understands   2/3 = unsure   0–1 = does not know

D.   Sound Segmenting (Use sound boxes and four markers)

Say: Now I am going to say a word and see if you can say each sound slowly. Push a
marker into a box for each sound you hear while you say each sound. Practice with *no*.

1.   red   _____   _____

2.   fast   _____   _____

3.   time   _____   _____   Total _____/12

Total: 3/3 = understands   2/3 = unsure   0–1 = does not know

WHAT'S IN THIS CHAPTER FOR ME?

Early Childhood Teachers

Research has shown that a knowledgeable teacher is the key to effective instruction. Consequently, it is vital that you understand the terms and research findings in this chapter. Pay close attention to the findings on alphabetic and letter knowledge, and phonemic awareness. Ehri's stages of word learning are particularly important. You will no doubt have students on all of these different levels, and must utilize effective strategies for each level of development. Be sure to read the lessons on phonemic awareness as models of instruction, and copy the sound box in Figure 2.1 and the phonemic awareness assessment in Figure 2.3. Both will come in handy for developing and assessing students' phonemic awareness.

Middle Grade Teachers

Research has shown that a knowledgeable teacher is the key to effective instruction. Consequently, it is vital that you understand the terms and research findings in this chapter. Phonemic awareness may seem to be only associated with young children, but read Figure 2.2 to see how it has an impact on older students you may be teaching. Look closely as Ehri's stages of word learning. Your students who struggle with reading are probably in an earlier stage of development and could benefit from the teaching suggestions listed. Finally, reread the five principles of instruction. These can apply to any grade level.

Invention Specialists

Research has shown that a knowledgeable teacher is the key to effective instruction. Consequently, it is vital that you understand the terms and research findings in this chapter. As a teacher of students with special needs, be particularly aware of the principles in this chapter that govern your instruction. Look closely at Figure 2.2 for information about how a lack of phonemic awareness may be the cause of reading difficulties of some students. Also, pay close attention to Ehri's stages of word learning. The students who struggle with reading are probably in an earlier stage of development than is typical and could benefit from the teaching suggestions listed.

CHAPTER 3

LEARNING AND TEACHING ABOUT CONSONANTS

Mrs. Jewett is a veteran kindergarten teacher. On the day we observe her class, she begins by gathering students in the carpeted area of her room and directing their attention to the pocket chart next to her. It holds four name cards: Morgan, Conner, Hannah, and Kaitlyn. The names are written in blue, except for the first letters which are written in red. Mrs. Jewett reads the names aloud with special assistance from each of the namesakes. She then pauses and says with a puzzled voice, "Now wait a minute. How can Conner and Kaitlyn start with the same sound when Conner has a *C* and Kaitlyn has a *K*?" The children discuss this excitedly until Mrs. Jewett says, "I think *c* and *k* like to play a little game and say the same sound."

Then Mrs. Jewett introduces a new game called "Switcheroo Game." She takes her scissors and cuts off the first letters of each name card, puts the first letters at the bottom of the pocket chart, and switches the order of the name cards. Then she calls on a student to find the missing first letter and put it at the beginning of the name. When this is done, she asks all the students to put thumbs up if they think the name is right. She compliments the students for their efforts with positive, funny comments such as, "Your brains are almost too big to fit in your heads."

Mrs. Jewett also uses the opportunity to reinforce for the students that names begin with uppercase and not lowercase letters, and to distinguish consonants from vowels. She ends the lesson by telling the students that they will be working with four new names tomorrow.

Before you continue reading, take a moment to reflect on this lesson by considering these questions:

■ What do you think Mrs. Jewett wants the children to learn about letters and sounds?

■ How does she promote active involvement by the students?

■ What aspects of this lesson and this classroom are applicable for older students?

As you read about the classroom activities that are described in this chapter, continue to focus on both the understandings about letters and sounds that readers are developing and the ways in which teachers can promote active involvement in a meaningful context. Think about how these activities relate to the principles presented in the last chapter.

Most of the letters in the alphabet are consonants, so it makes sense to examine carefully the relationships between consonants and the sounds they make in written words. In this chapter, we will use the concepts of phonemes and graphemes to explain the different ways in which consonants can be combined: blends, digraphs, and clusters. We will also present a variety of instructional activities that build on the principles presented in the previous chapter.

☐ UNDERSTANDING CONSONANTS

There are 21 letters in the English language that are considered consonants and 25 distinctive sounds (phonemes) that they can make. Each consonant usually represents fewer sounds than a vowel does. The letter (grapheme) *b*, for instance, either represents the sound (phoneme) heard at the beginning of *ball*, or it is silent, as in *comb*.

When consonants come before a vowel in a syllable, they are called **onsets.** The *b* in *ball* is an onset, and so is the *t* in the second syllable of *return*. These onsets play a major part in word identification. A reader who correctly recognizes the onset of a word stands a good chance of identifying the entire word.

Because most single consonants such as *d* always make the same sound, and because most words start with a consonant, they are generally the graphophonemic cues that beginning readers rely on first and most. Readers need to be aware, however, that consonants can make multiple sounds or can be silent. Three of the consonants, *c*, *q*, and *x*, actually have no phoneme of their own.

MULTIPLE SOUNDS

Mrs. Jewett was wise to introduce her students early to the notion that different letters can stand for the same sound and that the same letter can make different sounds. Beginning readers, as well as English language learners who can already read in their own language, may need teacher guidance to understand the following:

C borrows the /k/ sound in words such as *cat* and *cotton* to make the hard sound of *c*. The other sound that *c* can make is the soft sound /s/ as in *cent* and *cedar*.

Q makes no sound on its own, but is always paired with *u* and makes a /kw/ sound such as in *quick* and *queen*.

X is especially tricky. It can sound like /gz/ as in *exit*. It can sound like /ks/ as in *six*, or like /z/ as in *xylophone*. In words such as *x-ray*, we are saying the name of the letter *x* and not actually pronouncing the phoneme. In recent years, people pronouncing words such as *extreme* have tended to emphasize the letter *x* and made it sound like a phoneme, but technically, *x* is still a letter without its own sound.

G has a hard sound in words such as *gum* and *go*, but also can mimic a /j/, the soft sound of *g*, as in *giant* and *gym*.

S usually makes the /s/ sound in *sun* and *so*; however, *s* can also stand for the /sh/ phoneme in words such as *sugar*. *S* can also sound like /z/ in *is*.

Y is a particularly problematic letter. Many people say it is both a consonant and a vowel, but that is somewhat misleading. The sound in English that is unique to *y* is the consonant sound of /y/ as in *year*. *Y* can be a grapheme for the vowel phonemes /e/ and /i/ as in *funny* or *sky*, but it does not have its own vowel sound.

SILENT CONSONANTS

Whereas some consonants have multiple sounds, some make no sound at all. Say the following words aloud and identify which consonants are silent.

thumb   write   ghost   knife   walk   listen   wrong   salmon

People pronounce words differently. Regional differences, ethnic backgrounds, and other factors influence the way we speak, making it even more difficult to make hard and fast rules about phonics and pronunciation. Try saying the following words aloud.

often   *folk*   *calm*

Did you pronounce the *t* in *often*? Did you say the *l* in *folk* or *calm*? Some people will swear they do, but others are equally sure they do not. Neither answer is wrong. You are simply confirming the influence of your background and environment. Many consonants that we consider silent were pronounced by early speakers of English (Savage, 2004). Although the sounds have faded from our speech, the words remain a problem in our spelling.

Silent letters also appear in double-letter words. In the words *buzz, miss,* and *purr,* the second double letter is considered silent. When double consonants appear in the middle of a two-syllable word, this presents a more difficult situation. Some linguists (Fox & Hull, 2002) consider the second double consonant in words such as *summer, dinner, puppet,* and *puddle* also silent; however, because the first letter ends the first syllable and the second letter begins the second syllable, it would be more useful for students to consider them as separate sounds.

☐ LEARNING ABOUT CONSONANTS THROUGH SORTING ACTIVITIES

Students can begin to learn about the typical sounds of consonants and their variations through sorting activities. Sorting pictures or words can help children to focus on the similarities and differences between words. Sorting is, therefore, an excellent way to promote phonemic awareness. Bear et al. (2004) argue that word sorting is better than doing worksheets, because it involves more analytic thinking and many more examples can be done in a shorter period of time.

PICTURE SORTING FOR PRIMARY STUDENTS

One of the best ways to help emergent readers (those at the prealphabetic stage) to make letter-sound associations is to have them match letter names with pictures of objects that begin with that sound. To do picture sorts, make a set of cards with the targeted consonant letters on them. Then cut out pictures of objects that begin with those consonants and glue them onto poster board. Do not write the name of the picture on the card, because then children would visually match the beginning letter of the word to the letter card rather than think about sounds.

For increased durability, laminate or cover with clear contact paper. You can find pictures in phonic workbooks, but another more up-to-date source is clip art on computer programs such as Microsoft® Word or PowerPoint. It is important that the pictures are ones that students can clearly identify. For example, a child today is unlikely to recognize a picture of a top.

Place the cards in a large, labeled business envelope and include an answer key in a separate envelope with a clasp. Show the students how to take out the cards, arrange them under the letter that represents the beginning sound, and then check their own work.

WORD SORTING FOR INTERMEDIATE AND MIDDLE GRADE STUDENTS

Word sorting is a simple but highly versatile instructional activity for older readers at the phonemic stage of word learning or above. Students are simply asked to look closely at a group of words and to create subgroups that have a particular characteristic in common. For example, students might sort out those words that contain silent consonants, or those that end with the same sound. Remember that they should be sorting by the sounds they hear in the words rather than by their visual features.

Figure 3.1 shows how word sorting can be applied to initial consonant sounds in content area vocabulary. Notice that the list of words includes both words in which the grapheme c makes the /s/ phoneme and words where it makes the /k/ phoneme. For younger children, the directions might be exactly the same even though the words might be simpler and the consonants might not have multiple sounds. The words can also be written on cards and physically sorted out into piles.

■ FIGURE 3.1   Sorting Consonant Sounds

Can you sort these content area words by the sounds of their beginning consonants?			
gamma	citadel	chlorophyll	genocide
circumference	climate	cathedral	cytoplasm
gallon	gene	citizen	cell
colony	centimeter	culture	composite
germination	comet	condensation	genetics
century	circular	commutative	gorge
graph	congruent	capacity	geography
civilization	cyclical		
/k/	/s/	/g/	/j/

☐ CONSONANT BLENDS AND THREE-LETTER CLUSTERS

A **consonant cluster** is two or more consonant letters that blend together when sounded. These are more commonly called **consonant blends.** There are many examples of these in the English language. The most common consonant blends are formed with *l* (such as *black, clean, flag, glad,* and *place*) or *r* (as in *brush, crowd, drain, fresh, grape, press,* or *track*). Many blends begin with an *s* (such as *score, smart, sky, slide, snow, sport, stop,* and *swim*). Less common blends include *tw (twin)* and *dw (dwarf)*. Since *q* is always written with a *u* and makes a /kw/ sound, *qu* is considered a consonant blend.

There are also three-letter clusters (blends) that occur at the beginning of words such as *scrape, sprain, straight,* and *splash.* Although the phonemes are blended when the word is pronounced, the letters in a consonant blend are still considered to have separate sounds. In other words, you can still hear the individual /g/ and the /r/ sounds in the word *grape;* however, the sound at the beginning of *grape* should be considered different from the sound at the beginning of *gap*.

ENDING CONSONANT BLENDS

Consonant blends can be found at the end of words as well as at the beginning. For example, *st* can be at the beginning of *star* and at the end of *fast; sk* can be found in *skate* as well as *risk*. Some blends, however, are only found in the ending position of a word such as *-lt* in *salt, -mp* in *lump, -nd* in *friend, -ld* in *cold, -lk* in *milk, -nt* in *sent,* and *-ft* in *sift*. As readers develop, they learn more about variations and exceptions in the usual patterns of consonant sounds, and they gain experience with the ways in which consonants can be combined. In the middle grades, students can learn about clusters of consonants that come into English from other languages and apply that learning both to spelling and to identifying words that they encounter in content areas or in their independent reading.

The consonant cluster *ps*, for instance, is rarely seen in books for young children, but middle grade students may certainly encounter it, so it may be appropriate to embed a brief discussion of this cluster during a content area lesson about psychology or as a brief mini lesson during a literature discussion. Students may find it useful to note that this cluster comes to English from the Greek, and that it is always pronounced as /s/.

A teacher can help older students to see the connection between sound and meaning by pointing out that when the *ps* combination is found with a *y*, as it is in *psychotic*, the resulting word will probably have something to do with the mind or spirit. Students could be asked to name other words that they know that begin with *ps*. They could also do a quick dictionary search and add

■ **FIGURE 3.2** Reading and Writing Blends

To give students with limited literacy skills a more authentic experience in reading and writing words with blends, try the following:

1. Ask students to think up tongue twister sentences that use blends. An example might be, "The sled slid down the slippery hill."
2. Write the sentence on the board but leave spaces where the blends belong. Have the students come up and fill in the missing letters.
3. As students become more proficient, make sentences with many different blends in one sentence and sentences with missing ending blends such as, "He was sick after he drank pink ink."

one or more *ps* words to a word wall or personal spelling list. Learning about consonants may begin early, but it never really ends.

LEARNING ABOUT BLENDS THROUGH INDEPENDENT AND GUIDED ACTIVITIES

Teachers can help students to apply their knowledge of blends when writing independently by coaching them to stretch out the sound of the word they are trying to write as they pronounce it aloud. This "rubber banding" technique helps students to hear the individual sounds that are blended in the word.

Figure 3.2 shows a more teacher-directed activity in which students are guided to dictate sentences that contain blends and then practice filling in the blends in the text the teacher has written.

☐ CONSONANT DIGRAPHS

Whereas consonant blends make individual sounds, **consonant digraphs** are two-letter combinations that make only one sound. The most common consonant digraphs are easily recognized by the *h* as their second letter: *ch, sh, th, ph, gh,* and *wh*. *Ch, gh, sh,* and *th* can be both initial and ending digraphs. Sometimes both are found in the same word, as in *church*. Some linguists do not consider *ph* or *gh* digraphs because they represent the /f/ sound and not a unique sound as do the other digraphs. Digraphs, like single consonants, often represent more than one sound, and the sounds they make can sometimes be made in other ways:

> *Ch:* The most common sound of *ch* is the one heard at the beginning of *change;* however, it can also represent the /sh/ phoneme as in *champagne,* and the /k/ sound as in *chemical.*

Sh: The grapheme *sh* is quite reliable. That is, when a word is spelled with *sh* such as in *shell,* you can expect it to make the /sh/ sound. However, other graphemes can stand for the /sh/ phoneme. For example the *s* in *sure* makes a /sh/ sound; the *ch* in *machine* also makes a /sh/ sound, as does the *ti* in *action.*

Gh: The grapheme *gh* can represent two different single sounds. When it appears at the beginning of a word such as *ghost,* it makes a /g/ sound, but when it is at the end of a word, it has a /f/ sound as in *laugh.*

Wh: The /wh/ phoneme is a sound that has almost disappeared in American English pronunciation. The beginning of *white* and *way* sound the same to us, yet the differences in spelling remain. It is not helpful to ask students to listen to the beginning of a *wh-* word when pondering how to write it. Unfortunately, many common words have this spelling, such as *what, where, why, while, when* (*who* has an /h/ sound), so these words are better learned through sight and context cues.

Th: Th presents a problem for readers, because there are really two *th* sounds. The first is called the voiced *th* and it is shown with a slash across it [t͡h]. This represents the sound heard in words such as *there* and *that.* When we pronounce these words, our vocal chords vibrate. The other *th* phoneme is called unvoiced or voiceless *th.* Our vocal chords do not vibrate when we pronounce words such as *thin* and *thumb.* If you are having trouble hearing the difference, try the exercise shown in Figure 3.3.

■ **FIGURE 3.3   Voiced and Unvoiced TH**

Directions: First, put your fingers on your throat so you can feel your vocal chords. Then read down the list of words aloud, also paying attention to the position of your teeth and tongue as you say the words. Do you feel a difference between the voiced and unvoiced words? Now put your hand in front of your mouth so you can feel the air escaping from your mouth. This time, read across the list, back and forth between voiced and unvoiced. What differences do you feel?

Voiced th	Unvoiced th
than	thaw
the	theft
that	theatre
their	theme
them	thick
themselves	thief
then	thimble
there	thin
these	thing
they	think
this	third
those	thirsty
though	Thursday

☐ CLASSROOM ENVIRONMENTS FOR TEACHING CONSONANTS

Especially in the primary grades, teachers can create environments that surround students with reminders of what they are learning about letters, words, and sounds. They can also make sure that a variety of materials are at hand that allow students to manipulate letters and sounds. Some of the ideas described in this section can also be adapted for classrooms in the middle grades or for resource rooms.

NAME WORD WALL

Anyone who has taught young children knows that their names are important to them. They enjoy hearing their names and seeing them in writing. Teachers can take advantage of this by creating a name word wall, as shown here. The children's names are written on cards and posted under the beginning letters above the chalkboards around the classroom.

The teacher can refer to and use the names on a regular basis, making such connections as "The word *many* starts the same as *Marcus* and *Marissa*." This can also be an excellent way to point out the multiple spellings of phonemes,

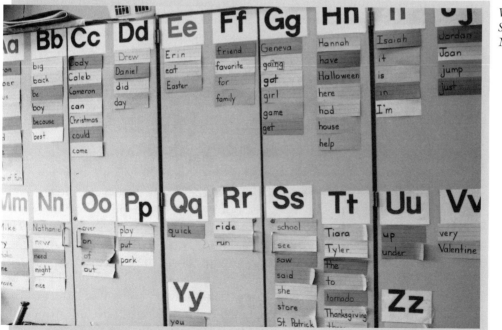

Word Wall with Students' Names.

such as *Shawna* and *Cheyanne*. The name word wall can also be used for ongoing informal assessment. A teacher might, for example, find out about students' knowledge of digraphs by asking an individual or group to look at the wall and find three different names that have a /ch/ sound.

LEARNING CENTERS

Learning centers are areas set up around the classroom that allow students to independently practice skills previously taught by the teacher. Typically, students work in the centers while the teacher is conducting reading groups. A study by Tracey and Morrow (1998) found that using literacy centers to reinforce phonic skills is highly motivating to children.

A letter and word study center could include a variety of books and other print materials such as children's magazines, telephone books, menus, product labels, and signs, as well as materials for creating words (e.g., magnetic letters, pens, pencils, markers, different kinds of paper and notepads, letter stamps and ink pads, typewriters, and computers). Students learning about consonants might be asked to find words beginning or ending with certain consonants or clusters in newspapers or magazines. They could be asked to find clip art pictures on the computer and group them according to consonant sounds. Older students could be asked to write a poem using as many words with blends, digraphs, or silent letters as possible.

Fountas and Pinnell (1996) suggest introducing centers one at a time, giving explicit directions and modeling for children how to do the activities at the center. Additionally, students must have all the materials they need to complete the activities, and procedures must be established and practiced concerning how to use and clean up materials.

ALPHABET BOOKS

Every literacy center should have a collection of high-quality alphabet books for students to read and enjoy. Even an emergent reader can have an independent reading experience by using the picture cues as aids. Many unusual and award-winning alphabet books have been published in recent years, but teachers must select books that match their goals. For example, *The Graphic Alphabet* (1995), *Alphabet City* (1995), and *The Butterfly Alphabet* (1996) feature beautiful letters that occur naturally in the environment, but the shapes of the letters are somewhat distorted or unclear. These would not be the best models for a student who is just beginning to recognize letters of the alphabet, but would present a nice challenge for students who are proficient. Likewise, the book *Tomorrow's Alphabet* (1996) proclaims that "A is for seed," very confusing for students trying to make sound-symbol connection, until they read "tomorrow's apple." Once again, this book would be a great tool for prediction but may not meet the objective of associating sounds with letters. Teachers also have to be aware of confusing concepts in some alphabet books. The book *C is for Curious* (1990) emphasizes the first letter of various emotions but chooses to use *xenophobic* for *x* and *zealous* for *z*.

Nonetheless, with careful selection, teachers can provide various alphabet books to serve as models for independent activities. One idea would be for students to create their own alphabet books by providing magazines, scissors, glue sticks, and blank books or spiral notebooks. The students would be directed to find or draw at least one picture for each letter. In the case of *x*, allow students to find a word with an *x* in it.

A more high-tech version of an alphabet book can be created on a computer by using a children's publishing program such as Kid Works Deluxe. Students can click on clip art and then type the beginning letter of the selection. This program has the additional benefit of the computer pronouncing the name of the picture the child has selected, making it even more motivating.

TAKE-HOME MAGNETS

Fox (2003) suggests a clever way for students to create their own set of letter magnets, which can be used to reinforce home–school connections while practicing letter sounds. Students are given 1-inch strips of adhesive magnetic tape and 2-inch pieces of poster board for each consonant letter or blend. In their literacy centers, students write the letter names on the poster board pieces, and assemble the magnets. The students then take home the magnets along with a letter from the teacher explaining different ways to use them. For example, a different letter magnet could be put on the refrigerator every day and the student would have to say a word (or a food that could be found in the refrigerator) that begins with that letter.

Several letters could also be posted and the child would go on a scavenger hunt in the house bringing back an object that begins with each of the letters. Once the child becomes more proficient at identifying consonant sounds, letter magnets with vowels could be added and students could be reading and writing words on their refrigerators every day.

GAMES TO REINFORCE CONSONANT SOUNDS

Games are also a wonderful way to review previously taught skills. These games can be done in small groups or whole class settings. Some games can be self-checking, but most are designed to have a teacher or aide serve as the guide. Because playing games is already motivating, students should not receive rewards for winning. Instead, everyone should be complimented for playing well and showing evidence that they have learned a skill. A good game should have a combination of skill and luck so that everyone has an equal chance of doing well.

BOARD GAMES Some board games can be too long and tedious for young children to play. When creating a game that asks players to move along a path to the finish, limit the number of spaces on the board to make the game go faster. Classic board games such as Candy Land and Chutes and Ladders can be adapted for students to practice consonant letters and other sounds simply by putting pictures on the board and having students roll a die and tell the first letter of the picture where they land. Another way to move along a board is to have students draw cards with letters and then move to the closest space with a picture that begins with that letter. An example of this type of game that reviews the three sounds of *y* is the teacher-made Bunny Hop game shown below.

Another type of board game is Bingo which can be adapted to use sound and picture matches. Even young children can learn to play and conduct simple games like this without adult supervision. You can add interest to an ordinary game like Bingo by tying it to a book or favorite author.

A Game to Practice the Multiple Sounds of Y.

CARD GAMES   Card games can also be somewhat difficult for young children to manage. The game should be set up so that students' hands have no more than four cards at a time, unless students can lay the cards face up in front of them. Card games are a real favorite of older students, and these games have the extra advantage of not taking up much storage space. Again, simple card games like Old Maid and Go Fish can be adapted to review phonics skills. In the case of consonant sounds, students can match cards marked with onsets with pictures that begin with those onsets. Students can also play a simple rummy game in which they pick up cards and then discard. Be sure to have multiple pictures that begin with an onset so that students have more than one chance to match the letters they hold in their hands.

ACTIVE GAMES   Students particularly enjoy games that involve physical activity. The game Twister can be adapted to practice consonant sounds by writing onsets on the colored spaces of the floor mat. When the players spin the color spinner, they must say a word that begins with the onset for that space before they can touch it.

Another active game is a relay race in which students must pass an object with an onset written on it to another student who must say a word beginning with that letter before passing it on to the next person.

Musical chairs is another physically active game that can be adapted to reinforce letter sounds. Tape papers with onsets written on them to the back of chairs (one less than the number in the group) and arrange them in a circle. The students move around the outside of the chairs while music is playing. When the music stops, the students must say a word that begins with the onset before they can sit in the chair. When students are eliminated, they become assistant judges so that they remain active participants in the game.

These are just a few of the many center activities and games that can be used to review phonics. Many more ideas will be presented in subsequent chapters. Although these activities might be perceived as merely ways to make learning more fun, they also have a more serious objective, which is to increase automaticity of word recognition and spelling so that students can focus on getting meaning from print.

☐ ASSESSING CONSONANT LETTERS AND SOUNDS

Principle 5 states that teachers must guide their instruction of phonics through ongoing assessment. Classroom assessment does not have to look or feel like a test, however. The best assessments are often informal and authentic, meaning that they are very much like the kinds of activities that are done daily in class. Informal assessment can be done individually or during group activities. Assessing an individual student's knowledge of letters and sounds can be done easily through an activity using letter cards. Simply buy a set of alphabet letters (or make your own on the computer) and prepare a chart like this:

LETTER	NAME	SOUND	WORD

Show each letter card to the student, making sure to present them in random, not alphabetical, order, and ask the student to identify the letter, make the sound of the letter, and say a word that begins with that letter. Include both uppercase and lowercase forms of each letter, and the two ways *a* and *g* are written in books. Record each student's responses on the chart.

Teachers can review the charts with individuals to discuss goals for further learning. They can also use them to form small groups for further instruction. By tallying responses, the teacher can obtain a profile of the whole class which can be used to plan activities that respond to student needs. Notice that the same letter cards and chart that were used for the assessment could also be used for instruction by students working with a partner or small group. Another convenient and useful item for teaching and assessing letter recognition

Magnetic Letter Alphabet Chart.

is magnetic letters. Students could be asked to find and hold up a letter that begins a word said by the teacher or another student. Students could also be asked to pick a letter for a peer and challenge the person to say a word that begins with that letter.

☐ INTERVENTION WHEN STUDENTS STRUGGLE

The games and learning center activities described in this chapter can be motivating to students who struggle with reading and writing. The language experience technique is another way to help students with limited cognitive abilities, English language learners, or students with physical disabilities who find it difficult to write. With the language experience technique, the student dictates a story or personal narrative to the teacher who writes it in the child's exact language. The text can then by read multiple times by the student and teacher. The student is usually successful in reading the text because the story is in his or her own words. The teacher can then use the text as a basis for instruction. Beginning consonant blends and digraphs could be highlighted by the student, identified, and associated with their sounds. The words in the story could be written on cards and matched with the original text or mixed up and put back into order by the student. Language experience is both personal and meaningful to the student and has a tremendous potential for teaching and assessing literacy skills.

Approaches that emphasize a multisensory approach to word identification can also be effective. Research has shown that activities that utilize kinesthetic (movement) and tactile (touch) modalities, in addition to visual and auditory ones, are more likely to form connections in the brain and therefore be remembered. Figure 3.4 describes a novel way to use this approach.

☐ ☐ ☐ ☐ ☐

▨ BEFORE YOU MOVE ON

Check Your Understanding
To review terminology used in this chapter, try analyzing your own name by answering the following questions.

1. Print your name._____
2. How many graphemes are in your name? _____
3. How many phonemes are in your name? _____
4. How many consonant blends are in your name? _____

■ FIGURE 3.4   Shaving Cream Writing

The best activities for students are ones that incorporate all three learning modalities: visual, auditory, and tactile. Shaving cream writing is an easy way to incorporate all these modalities in an appealing way that students, especially ones with developmental delays, are bound to remember. To make this a successful experience, it is vital that teachers are well organized, have all materials at hand, and have a system for distributing and cleaning up materials.

1. Give each student a puff of shaving cream. (This activity can also be done with hot chocolate mix, sand, etc.). Direct students not to touch it until you are ready.
2. Ask the students to spread out the shaving cream on their desks until it is flat and smooth.
3. Say each word of a previously prepared list of words with different consonant letters and ask the students to write with their finger the beginning letter of the word.
4. Repeat the activity while listening for ending and/or middle letter sounds. Ask students to practice writing both uppercase and lowercase letters.
5. Get helpers to pass out paper towels and premoistened cloths to facilitate cleanup. (This activity is also a good way to clean off desks before an open house!)

5. How many consonant digraphs are in your name? _____
6. How many silent letters are in your name? _____
7. What is the onset of your first name? _____

Try analyzing the name of a partner who will, in turn, analyze your name. Compare papers to see if your answers agree.

WHAT'S IN THIS CHAPTER FOR ME?

Early Childhood Teachers

This chapter introduces terms that identify discrete phonic elements, such as consonant blends and digraphs, which you must know well in order to help students decode words. Note carefully how different letters can make the same sound and, conversely, how the same letter can produce several different sounds. Try the "Check Your Understanding" exercise with your name to see how well you can analyze consonant phonemes.

This chapter provides different ideas for your primary classroom such as picture sorts, alphabet books, take-home magnets, and several games. Think about incorporating a name word wall in your classroom, as shown earlier in the chapter, to take advantage of your students' interest in their own names.

Middle Grade Teachers

This chapter introduces discrete phonic elements such as consonant blends and digraphs. Note carefully how different letters can make the same sound and, conversely, the same letter can produce several different sounds. Try the "Check Your Understanding" exercise with your name to see how well you can analyze consonant phonemes.

Being aware of the variations and combination of consonant sounds can help you to identify features to emphasize when you are introducing vocabulary or coaching students' attempts to spell. Please note the suggestions for analyzing more difficult consonant clusters such as *ps*. The words in Figure 3.1 are content area words that your students may find a struggle, especially if they are unaware of the multiple sounds of *c* and *g*. Your students may also enjoy the challenge of attempting to write and then read their own tongue twister sentences as shown in Figure 3.2.

Intervention Specialists

This chapter introduces the discrete phonic elements such as consonant blends and digraphs that you must know well in order to help your students decode words. Note carefully how different letters can make the same sound and, conversely, how the same letter can produce several different sounds. Try the "Check Your Understanding" exercise with your name to see how well you can analyze consonant phonemes.

Students who find reading to be difficult will enjoy a variety of different activities as described in this chapter such as games, picture sorts, and alphabet books. Students with developmental delays often use beginning consonant letters as their primary cue for decoding words, so knowledge of consonant sounds is vital. A name word wall is also a valuable tool to help these students connect with print.

Give careful attention to the "Intervention When Students Struggle" section in this chapter. Language experience is a wonderful technique to teach literacy skills to students who have limited reading and writing abilities. It can be motivating to students to be able to read and learn from their own language.

CHAPTER 4

LEARNING AND TEACHING ABOUT VOWELS

Students in Mrs. Blair's multiage primary classroom take out the following large letter tiles from a big plastic tub in the center of the room: two *a*s, a *g, r, n, d*, and *m*. They spread out a large piece of paper on the floor and wait for Mrs. Blair's directions. They are ready to begin their word work.

Mrs. Blair asks them, "Who can find a one-letter word?" Several children hold up an *a*, and Mrs. Blair distinguishes between the letter *a* and the word *a*. Next, Mrs. Blair asks, "Who can make a chunk?" Once students have tried it with their letters, Mrs. Blair takes the letters *a* and *n* and puts them in a pocket chart.

"I'm going to take an *m* and put it in front of *an* and make *man*," she says while demonstrating. Then she takes a *d* card and flips it over to the capital letter side. "What word have I made now?" Mrs. Blair points out that *Dan* is a name and must have a capital letter. She then asks students to work a little more independently. "Who can make another three-letter word using the chunk *-an*?"

The students proceed to create more words with their letters. They begin to experiment and make longer words such as *and* and *rang*. Mrs. Blair asks students to use all of their letters to spell the "secret word," *grandma*. She reminds them that the word *grandma* was in their book, *The Doorbell Rang*. One student notices the -*an* chunk is also in the word *rang*. Another student notices that the word *an* is on their word wall.

Before you read the rest of this chapter, consider these questions:

- What do you suppose Mrs. Blair is trying to teach about vowel sounds?
- How is the instruction about vowels embedded or connected to other literacy activities?
- How does Mrs. Blair make use of the decoding by analogy approach that was introduced in Chapter 2?

Vowels in the English language can often be confounding to both beginning and experienced readers. In this chapter, we present basic terminology that is used to understand vowel sounds. We also describe a variety of instructional activities that can help all readers to master the mysteries of vowels.

UNDERSTANDING VOWELS

Using the five vowel letters, you can produce 19 different sounds. The letter *y* can stand for a consonant phoneme in a word such as *year*, but it is not a vowel phoneme because it does not produce its own vowel sound. As you saw in the previous chapter, most consonant phonemes are represented by only one or two graphemes, but a single page in a book might contain four or five different ways of representing the same vowel sound. The long /e/ sound heard in *he*, for instance, is represented by *i* in *macaroni*, by *ea* in *meal*, and by *ee* in *wheel*. Figure 4.1 helps to demonstrate the complexity of the English language.

Effective instruction in phonics requires a system for understanding and explaining this complexity. Some vowel phonemes can be understood by classifying them into categories such as short, long, and controlled. Combinations of vowels have been labeled as vowel digraphs or diphthongs. Vowels also can be understood by considering them as part of chunks, or rimes, in words.

SHORT VOWEL SOUNDS

Short vowel sounds are usually the first ones learned because they tend to appear in short, one-syllable words. **Diacritical marks** are used to show vowel sounds to aid pronunciation. Short vowels are marked with a **breve** (˘) above the vowel. Some dictionaries do not show marks to indicate a short vowel sound; instead, they may show a **respelling** next to a word to indicate how it is pronounced. For example, the word *quit* might be written either as *kwit* or *kwĭt*.

■ FIGURE 4.1   Surprising Sounds

The famous English playwright, George Bernard Shaw, railed against the inconsistencies of English spelling. To illustrate his point, he offered this famous nonsense word example: *ghoti,* claiming that it was pronounced *fish* because:

The *gh* makes an /f/ as in *laugh*

The *o* makes a short /i/ sound as in *women*

The *ti* makes a /sh/ sound as in *nation*

Shaw makes a good point even though no English words beginning with a *gh* have the /f/ sound. He left a large portion of his estate to try to make the English language more phonetically regular, but little has changed.

Try these word puzzlers. The answers are at the end of the chapter.

1. Can you think of a four-letter word in which the *u* sounds like a short *i*? (Hint: It describes all of us these days.)

2. Can you think of a common word with eight consonants and only one vowel? (Hint: It is what teachers should look for in their students.)

3. Try this: What do these names have in common: Cy, Ernest, Hugh, Phil, and Sonny?

4. Can you figure out the name of this country without its vowels? *STRL*

When pronouncing a short vowel sound, it is better to use a key word that contains that sound, rather than to pronounce it in isolation. For example, short *a* sounds like the *a* in *cat,* short *e* sounds like the *e* in *bed,* short *i* sounds like the *i* in *pig,* short *o* sounds like the *o* in *top,* and short *u* sounds like the *u* in *cup.* This is done to prevent distorting the individual sound by holding the sound too long (e.g., /u/ becoming "*uuuuhhhh*"). Using key words can also minimize the influence of regional differences in pronunciation. Even so, students may have trouble distinguishing the /e/ sound from the similar /i/ sound in words like *pen* and *pin.*

There are two spelling patterns that tend to produce short vowel sounds. The consonant, vowel, consonant (CVC) pattern is found in words like *hat* and *pot.* The consonant in the CVC pattern can also be a consonant blend or digraph, so words such as *scratch* and *brush* also have CVC patterns. The other spelling pattern that usually produces short vowel sounds is the VC pattern found in short words such as *at* and *itch.*

The CVC and VC spelling patterns also appear as syllables in multisyllable words. When a syllable ends in a consonant, it is called a **closed syllable.** For example, the word *pencil* consists of two closed syllables. Notice, however, that only the *e* is a short vowel sound, because the first syllable is accented and the second is not. Vowel sounds in an unaccented syllable tend to be distorted.

It is important to remember that these spelling patterns tend to produce short vowel sounds, but not in all cases; for example, words such as *was, car, now*, and *call* have CVC patterns but not short vowel sounds. In addition, when *i* is followed by *ght* as in *light* or when *i* or *o* is followed by the letters *ld* as in *wild* or *cold*, the vowel sound is long, not short.

RIMES

A **rime** consists of the vowel and the rest of the letters in a syllable. Wylie and Durrell (1970) found that rime chunks have a more consistent pronunciation than individual letter sounds and that helping students to group letters into familiar rime chunks improves their ability to read and write words (Goswami, 1998). In addition, Adams (1990) identified 37 rimes that can generate nearly 500 words. These very useful rimes (also called **phonograms** or **word families**) are listed here.

ack	ank	eat	ill	ock	ump
ail	ap	ell	in	oke	unk
ain	ash	est	ine	op	
ake	at	ice	ing	ore	
ale	ate	ick	ink	ot	
ame	aw	ide	ip	uck	
an	ay	ight	it	ug	

If we cull from this list rimes that tend to produce short vowel words, then we can produce the following list of rimes and key words that would be quite useful for beginning readers.

Rime	Key Word	Rime	Key Word	Rime	Key Word
-ack	back	-ick	sick	-ock	clock
-an	man	-ill	fill	-op	stop
-ap	tap	-ink	pink	-unk	junk
-ash	mash	-est	best	-uck	luck
-ank	bank	-ell	bell	-ump	jump

LONG VOWEL SOUNDS

Long vowel sounds are easy to remember because "they say their name." They are marked with a **macron** above the vowel letter (ā, for example). There are three spelling patterns that tend to produce long vowel sounds. The first is a CVCe, the lowercase *e* representing a silent /e/ as in *nīce*.

Because of the many words that fit this pattern and have long vowel sounds, it is certainly a pattern worth teaching, but teachers must also be aware of the many exceptions to this rule. Words such as *give* and *love* have the CVCe pattern, but do not have long vowel sounds.

The second spelling pattern that usually produces long vowel sounds is the CVVC pattern in words such as *heat*. Primary teachers often refer to this rule as: "When two vowels go walking, the first one does the talking." The most consistent vowel combinations for this rule are: *ai, oa, ee, ay,* and *ea*. However, the first vowel does not always do the so-called talking. Exceptions include *field, great,* and *niece* in which the second vowel is long; and *head* and *threat* in which the first vowel is short. In some words, like *vein* and *said,* the vowel combinations do not give any clue as to the pronunciation. What vowel sound do you hear in these words? Nonetheless, many words in English follow the CVCe pattern so it is well worth teaching.

The third common spelling pattern that often produces long vowel sounds is the CV pattern. Like the VC pattern, this pattern is often found in short words such as *no, she, hi, my,* and *be*. Words like *do* and *to* also fit the spelling pattern, but do not follow the long vowel rule.

Syllables that end in a vowel are called **open syllables.** The VC pattern usually produces a long vowel sound when found in multisyllable words. Examine the following list of multisyllable, content area words to identify open and closed syllables and whether they follow their vowel rules.

basin	demand	impeach	population
mitosis	concave	bias	climate
hybrid	data	frequency	nitrogen
adobe	homogeneous	revolution	global
osmosis	refugee	acute	degree

The words in Figure 4.2 are a reference for long vowel phonograms using the various long vowel spelling patterns.

MAKING WORDS: A WAY TO PRACTICE VOWEL PATTERNS

In the opening vignette, Mrs. Blair was guiding her students to do Making Words, a wonderful activity for practicing spelling patterns in words (Cunningham, 2000). This activity requires some preparation on the part of the teacher, but it is well worth the effort. To begin, select a "secret word" that has several different vowels and enough consonants to create numerous words from the letters. We suggest that you use a significant word from a story the students are reading, or a content area word to make the activity more meaningful. Next, write words that can be made using the letters from the secret word, listing them in order from the shortest and easiest to the longest and most complex. Group words with the same rime chunks; for example, the secret word *planets* could make the words *pat, sat, pet, set, net, pen, ten, tan, plan, Stan, sent, lent, plate,* and *slate*. These words could then be sorted into categories such as words beginning with consonants or blends; words with

■ FIGURE 4.2   Long Vowel Phonograms

-ace	face	-ule	rule	-oach	coach	-ice	nice	-each	beach
-ade	fade	-une	June	-oad	road	-ide	side	-ead	bead
-age	cage	-use	fuse	-oak	soak	-ight	night	-eak	leak
-aid	maid			-oal	goal	-ike	bike	-eal	deal
-ain	pain			-oam	foam	-ild	child	-ean	bean
-aint	paint			-oan	loan	-ile	while	-eap	leap
-ait	bait			-oast	coast	-ime	dime	-east	beast
-ake	cake			-oat	boat	-ine	fine	-eat	beat
-ame	game			-obe	robe	-ipe	ripe	-eed	seed
-ane	cane			-ode	code	-ise	wise	-eek	peek
-ape	shape			-oke	joke	-ite	bite	-eel	feel
-aze	haze			-ole	hole	-ive	five	-eep	sleep
				-ome	home			-eet	sweet
				-one	bone			-eeze	sneeze

rime chunks such as *-at*, *-en*, *-an*, *-ent*, and *-ate* or by CVC and CVCe patterns. Next, the teacher thinks of at least two **transfer words,** which are longer, more difficult words that contain the same chunks. For example, the word *rental* is a transfer word for *-ent* and *hibernate* is a transfer word for the *-ate* rime. Once planned, the Making Words lesson procedure is as follows:

1. Students receive (or make) letter cards with the letters from the secret word, mixed up.
2. The teacher asks the students to create the word that is pronounced, using the letters. A student can also arrange the letters on a pocket chart for everyone to see, but each student should also form the words with individual letters.
3. Students must use all of their letters to reveal the secret word.
4. Students now sort the words according to the sort categories.
5. The teacher introduces the transfer words and asks which words from the list would help the students to read these new words. This is done to encourage students to use familiar patterns to figure out new words.

Making and Writing Words (Rasinski & Padak, 2001) is a variation of Making Words created by Tim Rasinski, which is more appropriate for older students. Instead of using individual letter cards, students write the words on a sheet of paper. The teacher can give clues to each word, instead of telling the actual word to make it more challenging. For example, if the secret word is *America*, students write words using those letters, such as *crime* and *cream*, and then write transfer words such as *screaming*. This variation has the added benefit of providing a written record of the work.

OTHER VOWEL SOUNDS

CONTROLLED VOWELS   English vowels, unfortunately do not fall neatly into the categories of short and long. Some vowels are influenced by the consonants that follow them. The most notorious vowel controllers are *r, l,* and *w*. The following words have a vowel followed by an *r*. Can you sort them according to the different vowel sounds you hear?

car	her	forty	more	dirt	heart
scar	born	turn	dare	hear	beard
horse	myrrh	stir	work	chair	march
thirst	worm	scarf	short	prayer	burn
bear	spear	their	door	wear	share

You should have heard five different *r*-controlled vowel sounds. The first is the sound you hear in the word *dare*. The vowel sound would be identified in the dictionary with a ^ above an *a* (â). Notice the different spelling patterns that represent this sound: *-air, -ear, -are, -ayer, -ere,* and *-eir*. It is no wonder spelling this sound is a challenge for students! Equally as confusing is the vowel sound heard in *her*, which can be spelled with an *ir, or, ur, er, ear,* or even *yrr* in the case of *myrrh*. The diacritical symbol for this sound is a ^ above a *u* (û). The third *r*-controlled sound is the one heard in *car*. This is usually spelled with an *ar*, but more unusual spellings are found in words such as *bazaar, hearth,* and *are*. The dicritical marking is an *a* with two dots above it (ä), called an umlaut. The fourth *r*-controlled sound is usually spelled with *or* as in *born*, but can also have a *-oor* spelling as in *door* and *floor*. Note that this sound is different than the one made by *or* in words such as *worm* or *worse*. The final sound is most often spelled with *-ear* in words such as *hear* and *beard*. It is represented in the dictionary by an *i* with a ^ (î). It is important to note that not all vowels followed by *r* are changed. For example, in the word *wire*, the *i* retains the long /i/ sound. The age of the students will determine how much information about these vowels teachers should teach.

Certainly, even the youngest students need to be aware of "bossy *r*" words and how the vowels sound different than short and long ones. Somewhat older students can be "word detectives" and find words that sound the same but are spelled differently. Older students can be taught how to use dictionary pronunciation guides and respellings to decipher vowel sounds on their own.

■ FIGURE 4.3 Controlled Vowel Phonograms

-air	fair	-ear	dear	-ir	stir	-oar	roar	-ull	dull
		-ear	bear					-ull	full
-alk	talk	-eer	deer	-ird	bird	-oll	doll	-ur	fur
-all	ball	-erge	merge	-ire	tire	-olt	colt	-ure	cure
-alt	salt	-erk	jerk	-irk	shirk	-oor	poor	-urn	burn
-ar	car	-erm	germ	-irt	shirt	-or	for	-urse	nurse
-ard	hard	-ern	fern	-irth	birth	-orch	porch	-urt	hurt
-arge	large	-erve	nerve			-ord	cord		
-ark	park					-ore	sore		
-arm	farm					-ork	fork		
-arn	barn					-orn	born		
-art	part					-ort	short		
-aw	saw					-our	sour		
-awl	crawl								
-awn	lawn								

Vowel phonemes can also be influenced by the letters *l* and *w*. The following list of words fits into this category.

raw	walk	tall	talk	saw
awful	almost	shawl	law	pull

The same vowel sound heard in the previous words is also found in the next words, with different spelling patterns.

taught	broad	caught	fought	Paul

This vowel sound is represented by an *o* with a ^ (ô).
The respelling of *caught* would look like this: *kôt*.
Figure 4.3 provides examples of controlled vowel phonograms.

VOWEL DIPHTHONGS   A **vowel diphthong** is defined as a single vowel phoneme that is written with two letters that represent a gliding sound between the vowel sounds. There are two vowel diphthong phonemes, but there are four graphemes that represent them. The first phoneme is the /oi/ sound found in words like *boil, toy, foil,* and *employ*. Notice that the sound can be spelled with an *oi* or an *oy*. The second vowel diphthong phoneme is /ou/ heard in such words as *loud, cow, shout,* and *scowl*. In this case, the sound is spelled with *ou* or *ow*. Care should be taken to distinguish the diphthong sound found in *cow* with the long vowel sound found in *row* and *low*. Once again, context is critical to determining the pronunciation and meaning of certain words. For example, the word *bow* could mean a fancy ribbon on a gift, a formal gesture, or the front of a ship, depending on the sentence.

VOWEL DIGRAPHS   **Vowel digraphs** are two-letter vowel combinations that represent only one vowel phoneme. Vowel pairs such as *oa, ai, ay,* and *ee* are technically vowel digraphs because they produce only one sound; however, these long vowel sounds are more understandable when students group them with other long vowel patterns. We prefer to distinguish these vowels from others that make one unique sound. Therefore, the only vowel combination that meets this criterion is the *oo* letter combination, but *oo* can stand for two distinctive sounds. First is the phoneme heard in words such as *food* and *spool.* The diacritical marking for this vowel sound is called an elongated macron ($\overline{oo}$). The second phoneme is the sound heard in *look* and *stood*. In the dictionary, these words would be marked with an elongated breve ($\breve{oo}$). This phoneme is usually represented by the *oo* grapheme, except in words such as *could, would,* and *should,* where it is spelled with a *ould*. The first *oo* phoneme is even more problematic. This same sound is found in words with a great variety of spellings such as *do, grew, soup, through,* and *clue.* In fact, many words that we think of as long *u*, silent *e* have, in actuality, a /oo/ phoneme (e.g., *tune, cube, mule*). To make matters even more complicated, not all words spelled with *oo* have a vowel digraph sound: In the word *blood,* the vowel phoneme is short *u*.

Figure 4.4 provides vowel diphthong and digraph phonogram examples.

■ **FIGURE 4.4**   **Vowel Diphthongs and Digraph Phonograms**

-ouch	couch	-oil	boil	-oo	boo	-oose	goose
-oud	loud	-oin	coin	-ood	food	-oot	foot
-ounce	bounce	-oise	noise	-ood	good	-ooth	tooth
-ouse	house	-oy	toy	-oof	goof		
-out	shout			-ook	book		
-outh	mouth			-ool	cool		
-ow	cow			-oom	boom		
-owl	growl			-oon	moon		
-own	down			-oop	hoop		

SCHWA SOUNDS   Vowels found in unaccented syllables are more likely to be distorted and not as easily classified as long, short, or any of the other vowel phonemes. The term given to nondistinct vowels in an unaccented syllable is a **schwa** sound, represented by a symbol that resembles an upside-down *e* (ə). The schwa phoneme most often sounds like *uh* in multisyllable words, such as the *a* in *about*, but it can also make other sounds. The second syllable vowels in each of the following words is considered a schwa sound: *pencil, button,* and *pizza,* but each is spelled with a different letter and each makes a slightly different sound. It is not important that children know the different schwa sounds; rather, they should realize that they may not be able to clearly hear all the vowel sounds in multisyllable words. This will have an impact on student spelling, especially at the middle grade level where longer, technical words are used more frequently. A teacher needs to make the decision whether these words are better learned by breaking them down into syllables and using the compare/contrast method, or relying on context and syntax cues. In the following word list, what kinds of vowel sounds do you see? How would you help students pronounce them and spell them?

countenance	rarified	mercenary	insurrection
formidable	adversary	spurned	Spartan
contentious	plausible	crooked	subservient
perpendicular	grousing	augment	disproportion
annoyance	infirmity	cloister	brooding

☐ WHOLE CLASS TEACHING AND LEARNING ACTIVITIES

WORD WALLS

A **word wall** is a classroom display of words actively taught by the teacher and used by the students to aid reading and writing. Word walls that feature sight words are the most common ones found in classrooms today, but another kind of word wall, called a **chunking word wall,** helps students use common rime chunks to compare and contrast new words. The teacher introduces a chunk such as -*an* and guides the students to create words by adding different onsets. Once a list of words has been created, the students and teacher choose a key word, such as *man,* to represent that chunk. This word is written on a card and put on the word wall. The words on the word wall are reviewed daily using fun activities such as Guess the Secret Word, in which students are given clues and must narrow them down to the secret word. The teacher constantly makes reference to words on the word wall. For example, when a familiar chunk appears in a text, the teacher points it out and encourages students to find other examples. Also, when students are engaged in independent writing, they should correctly spell words with chunks from the word wall, for example, the

■ FIGURE 4.5   A Glimpse into the Classroom: Mrs. Katie Steffen

First-grade teacher Katie Steffen introduces her students to different rime chunks each week. The students practice changing the onsets to create new words and generate words containing the chunk. Then the students choose a key word, which she calls a "rainbow word," to go on their class word wall. This word is put up with Velcro so that if students need it in their writing, they can remove it and then replace it. Mrs. Steffen consistently refers to the words and encourages students to find rainbow words in other contexts such as in signs, poems, Big Books, or other texts for reading groups. The rainbow words also become the students' weekly spelling words. In this way, Mrs. Steffen combines reading and writing skills by teaching students familiar word patterns.

word *than*. Figure 4.5 tells how first-grade teacher Katie Steffen incorporates her word wall with reading and writing instruction.

BRAND NAME PHONICS

The Brand Name Phonics activity developed by Patricia Cunningham (2000) is a creative and motivating way to help students focus on rime chunk patterns. The teacher uses the actual brand labels from household products to introduce a rime. For example, a *Crest* label could be used to show the -*est* chunk. Other words are then generated that have the same chunk, such as *best, nest, rest,* and *west*. Finally, more difficult words with that chunk can be read and written such as *contest* and *conquest*. Students enjoy finding their own labels and making their own compare and contrast lists.

WORD SORTS

Word sorts are done simply by classifying words into different categories. This classification requires real analysis on the part of the learner, and results in several kinds of sorts. In a *closed sort,* the teacher designates the categories, for example, short vowel and long vowel words. The teacher can control the complexity of the task by limiting the words given to only one-syllable short or long vowels, or may by choosing to make the sort more challenging by adding an "other" category and words that have different vowel sounds. The second type of sort is an *open sort,* in which students must decide for themselves how to classify the words. Examine the following words and decide what sort categories you could create. Would you ask students to do an open or closed sort?

box	made	with	his	and
be	road	hot	paid	Chris
Tony	meet	we	happy	Kate

Another kind of word sort is the *speed sort,* where students try to sort the words as quickly as possible. This helps to promote automaticity in reading and spelling. In a *blind* or *spelling sort,* students are not told the categories and the words are dictated to them. Students must decide whether to classify and write each word with the previous category or to start a new one. This is a particularly good sort to use with middle grade students.

WORD LADDERS

Word ladders are created by changing only one letter in a word to make a new word. Rasinski and Padak (2001) created a word ladder that changes *snow* into *rain*: snow–show–shoe–hoe–hole–mole–male–ale–ail–mail–main–rain. Depending on the level of the students, these words could be dictated to them or cues to their meaning could be given. Can you create a word ladder for your students changing *walk* into *run?*

ONSET AND RIME WRITING

The Onset and Rime Writing activity is simple for a whole class or small group, but it requires quick thinking on the part of the teacher. Beforehand, the teacher prepares a deck of cards with different onsets on each. The teacher then tapes to the class board four to five rime chunks that students are to practice. Next, the deck of onsets is passed out to each student. The students come up to the board and try to write as many words as they can make combining their onset with the rime chunks. If the students cannot make a real word, they are permitted to write a nonsense word. Not knowing beforehand what words the students will write, the teacher must be able to think quickly when working with the words. The words should be read aloud. The students should identify which words are nonsense ones, but the teacher should point out that these "Dr. Seuss" type words could appear in a proper name or part of a multisyllable word, and are therefore worth decoding. The teacher should also instantly decide how to handle words that fit the spelling pattern but not the sound pattern, for example, if the word *said* is grouped with other *-aid* words. Once again, a clever teacher can turn this into a teachable moment to learn about exceptions to the rule. Finally, teachers can avoid potential embarrassment by removing onsets beforehand that could result in questionable words.

☐ SMALL GROUP GAMES

ONSET AND RIME BINGO

Players are given laminated cards divided into nine spaces with different rime chunks, in random order, and an overhead marker. The teacher chooses a card with an onset on it. If the student can make a real word with one rime chunk, then she or he writes the onset on the card before the rime. The first player to fill in all the spaces wins. Be sure to have wet paper towels available for cleanup.

RED LIGHT/GREEN LIGHT

Prepare a deck of cards for each competing student or group of students. The cards should have words with the same vowel letter, but different spelling patterns, for example, long *a* CVCe, short *a* CVC, long *a* CVVC, short *a* VC. The teacher writes these categories on the board. A student is then asked to roll *a* die. The number determines how many words need to be collected for each pattern and is recorded under that pattern. When the teacher says, "green light," students start turning over the cards in their deck. When they have collected all the necessary cards, students say, "red light," and the game stops. The cards must be checked before a winner is declared.

ROLL-A-VOWEL

Players are given a game card with words that have the vowels missing. Small cards with vowels on them are placed in the middle of the table. Players roll wooden dice (available at teacher supply stores) with the vowels written on them. If students can make a real word, they take one of the letters and put it on their card. The first player to fill the card wins.

MAKE-A-WORD

Players are given a game card, divided into nine sections, with a vowel or vowel combination in the middle and various onsets in the other spaces. Players place a marker on any onset. During each turn, a player can move only one space, in any direction. Players attempt to spell out a real word by combining an onset with a vowel chunk and then adding their own ending. When players make a word, they get a point for each letter in their word. The player with the most points wins.

SPILL-A-WORD

The teacher writes letters on the sides of six wooden cubes and assigns a point value to each according to frequency of use, for example, a = 1, x = 10. The cubes are placed in an empty potato chip tube or similar container. On their turn, players spill out the cubes and attempt to make as many words as possible in a set time. Another player will write the words and tally up the scores. The player with the most points wins.

Word Rummy

The teacher prepares a deck of onsets using one color card and a deck of rime chunks on a different color. The rime deck is placed down in the center with the top card turned up next to the deck. Each player then receives five onset cards. On their turn, each player chooses either the top card or the first face-down card in the deck. If players can make a real word, they take both cards out of their hand and say the word, and then discard. If players cannot make a word, they must pick a card from the deck and pass their turn. The player to match all of the cards first wins.

Rime Scattergories

Players are given a game sheet with lists of rime chunks. At the signal, they must write a word that has that chunk; however, players are only given points if their word is different than the other players' words. Therefore, students must quickly think of more difficult words, for example, *jig* instead of *big* for -*ig*. After a short time (2 to 5 minutes for primary and 1 to 2 minutes for middle grades), students compare their words with the others in the group. After three rounds, the person with the most unique (but not nonsense) words wins.

Content Area Vowel Rummy

This rummy game is most appropriate for middle grades. The teacher writes content area vocabulary words, which the students have been introduced to, on cards with spaces for the clear (not schwa) vowel sounds. With five cards in their hand, players must figure out what each word is, then arrange the cards according to the same vowel sound. The rest of the deck sits face down with one card up next to the pile. Each player picks either one unknown card from the deck or the entire discard pile. When a player collects three cards with the same vowel sound, she or he must say all of these words before laying them out on the table. The player who gets rid of all cards first wins.

☐ Interventions When Students Struggle

Teachers can use small groups or individual conferences to help students when they struggle with word identification. Imagine, for instance, that Mr. Simpson is holding a conference with Tina, a sixth grader who is struggling with reading her social studies book. Mr. Simpson asks Tina to find a sentence that is giving her difficulty and to read it aloud.

Tina reads, "The settlers met with Chief . . ." and then stops at the name Massasoit. She makes an /m/ sound and says, "I don't know that word."

Instead of telling Tina the word, Mr. Simpson says, "Do you recognize any chunks in the word?"

Tina looks at the word again and replies, "Mass, like Massachusetts where the Pilgrims landed."

"Good. What else do you see?"

"The last part, -*soit* sort of looks like *soil*."

"What would *soil* sound like if you substituted a *t* for an *l*?"

"*Soit*."

"Okay, now here's the tricky part. The *a* doesn't sound like a long or short *a*. It just makes an /uh/ sound. Now let's put the chunks together."

"Mass-uh-soyt."

Mr. Simpson then explains that Massasoit was chief of all the villages in the area. He ends the conference by reminding Tina that even if she cannot be entirely sure of the pronunciation of a difficult proper name like Massasoit, she can come close by using chunks from words she knows.

This brief scenario illustrates difficulties that vowel sounds may pose. Did you notice that the first *a* in *Massasoit* has a different sound than the second one? It also illustrates several important features of effective conferences.

- The teacher gives the student some responsibility for locating the source of the difficulty.
- Instead of giving answers, the teacher helps by giving Tina a specific strategy (looking for familiar chunks) that she can use to resolve the difficulty.
- By elaborating a bit on the content, the teacher makes it clear that the purpose of the reading is understanding the text rather than perfect word identification.
- The teacher communicates that difficulties are to be expected, but that there is always something a student can try in order to overcome them.

Students can also receive help from sources other than the teacher. See the appendix for a description of websites for students with special needs.

☐ ASSESSING VOWEL SOUNDS

By carefully observing students while they are engaged in the activities described in this chapter, a teacher can informally assess their knowledge of vowel sounds. For example, a primary student could be asked to independently sort a set of picture cards into piles according to the vowel sounds heard. A middle grade student might be asked to read words particularly chosen to represent the different vowel combinations or spelling patterns, such as *loyal* or *foolish*.

The following is an informal assessment of vowel phonemes using nonsense words. The reason nonsense words instead of real words are used is to ensure that the student is decoding the words rather than recognizing them from memory. The words become progressively harder and represent the major spelling patterns. Students should be asked to read the words aloud. The errors the student makes could be used to pinpoint areas of further instruction.

1. dat		15. plo
2. wep		16. ste
3. rin		17. twy
4. bom		18. swight
5. mub		19. scraw
6. blaid		20. sparm
7. clane		21. strore
8. grite		22. splurch
9. frope		23. skear
10. troag		24. sploush
11. snute		25. skairp
12. druim		26. scrook
13. smeeb		27. dwool
14. prean		

◻ ◻ ◻ ◻ ◻

BEFORE YOU MOVE ON

Summary of Vowel Sounds

The following table summarizes the vowel sounds and spelling patterns of the English language. Try thinking of another example of a word for each vowel sound and spelling pattern.

OTHER VOWEL COMBINATIONS		
SHORT VOWELS	PATTERNS: CVC, VC	CLOSED SYLLABLES
ă bat	match add	saddle
ĕ leg		
ĭ it		
ŏ not		
ŭ up		

OTHER VOWEL COMBINATIONS		
LONG VOWELS	**PATTERNS: CVCe, CV, CVVC**	**OPEN SYLLABLES**
ā cave	rate mail	table
ē sleep		
ī hi		
ō soap		
ū use		

OTHER VOWEL COMBINATIONS			
CONTROLLED	**DIPHTHONGS**	**DIGRAPHS**	**SCHWA [ə]**
â dare	oi/oy toy	o͞o food	pizza
û bird	ou/ow loud	o͝o book	
ä car			
î hear			
ô tall			

There are different graphemes that represent the same phoneme, and there are many exceptions to the so-called rules of phonics. Teachers need to be knowledgeable about the various vowel sounds and their exceptions in order to help students sort out the many peculiarities of English.

ANSWERS TO QUESTIONS IN FIGURE 4.1:

1. busy
2. strengths
3. They are all names that can be written differently as words: Cy = sigh, Ernest = earnest, Hugh = hue, Phil = fill, Sonny = sunny.
4. Australia

WHAT'S IN THIS CHAPTER FOR ME?

Early Childhood Teachers

This chapter contains critical information about vowel phonemes and vowel spelling patterns that you need to know to help students learn to decode words. Be sure to note examples of exceptions to these spelling patterns, and begin to practice analyzing words to see if they are phonetically regular. There are numerous teaching ideas in this chapter for early childhood teachers. Word walls, word sorts, and Making Words are particularly good strategies for primary students. Be sure to make use of the lists of common phonograms listed in this chapter. Read carefully how primary teachers Katie Steffen and Kate Blair teach rime chunks in their classroom. They provide excellent models of instruction.

Middle Grade Teachers

The classroom scenario in the "Interventions When Students Struggle" section illustrates how you might teach phonics and word identification, not as whole class lessons, but in individual "coaching" sessions with students. When students are confronted with difficult proper names, they have no other strategy than decoding to figure them out. This chapter contains critical information about vowel phonemes and vowel spelling patterns that you need to know in order to help students. Be sure to note examples of exceptions to these spelling patterns, and begin to practice analyzing words to see if they are phonetically regular. Brand Name Phonics and Making and Writing Words are both excellent activities to use with middle grade students. Many of the games described, especially Rime Scattergories, word ladders, and Content Area Rummy, are best suited for middle grade students.

Intervention Specialists

This chapter contains critical information about vowel phonemes and vowel spelling patterns that you need to know to help students. Be sure to note examples of exceptions to these spelling patterns, and begin to practice analyzing words to see if they are phonetically regular. Your students will find many of the teaching ideas in this chapter to be motivating and useful to their reading. Word walls, word sorts, and Making Words can all be adapted to be used at even the most emergent developmental level, as well as the games described. Read carefully the section "Interventions When Students Struggle" for ideas on how to coach students individually. Be sure also to check out the websites for students with special needs, as described in the appendix. Finally, consider using the nonsense word assessment in your classroom as a quick and easy survey of your students' knowledge of vowel phonemes and spelling patterns.

CHAPTER 5

Incorporating Phonics and Word Identification into Reading Instruction

Ms. Kelly is reading aloud to her first-graders from a Big-Book version of *Is Your Mama a Llama?* by Deborah Guarino (1989). Today is the third day in which she has read from this book. The children have especially enjoyed it for the repetition of the question, "Is your mama a llama?," which the lost baby llama asks each of his animal friends.

Each day, Ms. Kelly has drawn her students' attention to a different aspect of the book such as using the picture and rhyming word cues to predict which animal the baby llama will ask next. Today, she pauses when she reads the sentence:

"Oh," I said. That is certainly true. I think that your mama's a
_____."

Rather than saying the word *kangaroo*, Ms. Kelly lets the children supply the missing word. Then she says, "*Kangaroo* is a very long word. Let's count and see how many beats it has." The children all clap their hands three times as they slowly pronounce each syllable.

Ms. Kelly tells the students to listen to the beginning sound of the word *kangaroo* and asks, "What letter makes this sound?" The children eagerly raise their hands and everyone seems to recognize the letter *k*.

Then Ms. Kelly turns back to the book and points to the words *cow* and *cave*. "Do these words make the same beginning sound as *kangaroo?*" she asks. The children nod their heads, and Ms. Kelly says, "That's right. The /k/ sound can be spelled with a *c* or a *k*. Let's make a list of words that make that sound. You think of the words, and I'll write them."

Ms. Kelly takes a marker and divides a piece of chart paper down the middle. She writes *c* at the top of one column and *k* at the top of the other. The children begin to call out suggestions: *cat, kitten, can, cold, cook, kitchen, Kate,* and *come,* but before Ms. Kelly writes the word in the column, she asks students to raise their hands to show if they think the word begins with *c* or *k*.

The children enjoy this activity, and when they are done they notice that there are more words that began with *c* than *k*. Ms. Kelly reminds them to remember that when they are writing. She suggests that, if they are unsure, they should try the *c* first and see if the word looks right. If not, they should try a *k*.

Just then, Spencer raises his hand to say that he saw a *k* at the end of the word *think*. Ms. Kelly compliments Spencer for noticing this and says that when the /k/ sound comes at the end of a word, it is more likely to be spelled with an *-nk* as in *wink, stink,* or *rink* or a *ck* as in *lick, stick, luck, pack,* or *lock*.

Ms. Kelly ends the lesson by distributing individual copies of the book and asking students to read it in pairs. She instructs them that when they come to a word with a letter *c* or *k* to notice if it is in the beginning, middle, or end of the word and to write an example of each in their journals.

Before you continue reading, take a moment to reflect on this lesson by considering the following questions:

- How does Ms. Kelly incorporate both phonemic awareness and phonics instruction in this lesson?
- How does she help the students use other cueing systems?
- How does Ms. Kelly make the lesson meaningful to her students?

As you continue to read this chapter, consider the advantages and disadvantages of teaching phonics and word identification by using children's literature.

Take note of specific kinds of instruction you may want to use in your own classroom.

Teaching phonics and word identification within the context of reading and discussing literature is called **embedded** or **authentic instruction.** In this chapter, we will explore embedded instruction by presenting arguments that support its use and addressing important guidelines for using it successfully. We will also describe common ways to organize literature study so that phonics and word identification can easily be incorporated into small group and whole class learning activities.

☐ USING EMBEDDED INSTRUCTION

In the past, phonics has sometimes been taught via workbook pages and other skill and drill exercises, but many educators have found these activities to be of limited value for helping students become better readers (Stahl et al., 1998; Routman, 2000). Children using these materials may have become quite proficient at circling the picture that begins with a certain letter, but that did not necessarily transfer when they tried to read or spell a word on their own.

Embedded instruction does not mean that elements of phonics should never be taught in isolation. Sometimes it is helpful to focus on just one aspect such as the sound that short *a* makes, but as soon as possible, students must be able to use that information in a real reading context. As Routman (2000) argues, students should also be taught strategies for using skills independently in their own reading.

Tompkins (2003) believes there should be a balance between explicit and embedded instruction. Expanding on her thoughts, phonics is best learned in meaningful contexts. Ms. Kelly's lesson in the opening scenario is done with first graders, but it illustrates many of the ways in which effective teaching of phonics and word identification can be embedded in meaningful activities for readers of all ages.

PLANNING "SPONTANEOUS" LESSONS

Ms. Kelly has specific objectives in mind for her lesson. First, she wants her students to experience good children's literature with rich language, meaningful content, and a clear structure, so she chose *Is Your Mama a Llama?* Second, she wants to teach her students that the letters *c* and *k* can make the same hard /c/ sound; and third, she wants to give students a strategy for spelling words with this sound.

Ms. Kelly designed the lesson to actively involve the students and move them toward independence. She guides them to "discover" that *c* and *k* can make the same sound rather than just telling them, and she asks them to use their oral language knowledge to suggest words that begin with the /k/ sound. Notice that after the whole-class lesson, students are encouraged to apply the ideas during their partner reading. Finally, the lesson includes an example of the direct teaching of strategies when Ms. Kelly tells students how to use their knowledge about the /k/ sound when writing.

Although Ms. Kelly has carefully planned her lesson on beginning letter sounds, she did not anticipate that Spencer would notice a word with *k* in the final position. She recognized a "teachable moment," however, and quickly did a spontaneous mini lesson on this topic. In embedded approaches, the teaching of skills is not left up to chance or only taught spontaneously. Nevertheless, one of the great advantages of such approaches is that teachers can address questions that arise naturally out of reading and writing activities.

ENCOURAGING STUDENTS TO USE CUEING SYSTEMS

When Ms. Kelly paused during her oral reading to allow the students to supply the word *kangaroo,* she was inviting them to use the overall meaning of the story and the structure of the sentence, as well as the rhyme cue. In subsequent lessons, Ms. Kelly might turn to the page that describes a bat: "She hangs by her feet and she lives in a cave, I do not believe that's how a llama behaves." She could cover up the word *cave* with a sticky note and ask the students to use semantic cues to figure out the missing word by rereading the sentence and asking, "What word would make sense?"

Ms. Kelly could then encourage the use of multiple cues by writing the letter *c* on the note and asking, "Which of those words also begins with the letter *c*?" To remind them of syntactic cues, she could write three choices on the sticky note such as *cave, same,* and *house,* and ask, "Which word sounds right in the sentence?" She might also make deliberate errors during her oral reading of the book and have students tell her how they know the word is incorrect.

INCORPORATING PHONICS INSTRUCTION
IN SHARED READING

Ms. Kelly's lesson is one example of an approach to reading instruction called **shared reading.** Moustafa and Maldondo-Colon (1999) call shared reading "a powerful teaching strategy that enables early readers to become proficient readers." When using shared reading, children and the teacher read the text on multiple occasions. The first reading by the teacher is usually done to simply enjoy the book and to discuss personal reactions to it—in other words, to just appreciate it as children's literature. Subsequent readings focus more on specific aspects of the text, including graphophonemics.

Sharon Taberski (2000), a practicing New York City primary teacher, details specific strategies that she uses to do "letter and sound explorations" when engaged in shared reading. Her five steps are as follows:

1. Decide on the letter(s) or sound for which you want the children to search.

2. Start a list of words. These include words from the text and ones the children offer that they know.

3. Add to the list. Taberski explains to the children that if they come across a "particularly interesting" word during their own independent reading throughout the week, they can add it to the list.

4. Sort the words into categories to demonstrate similarities and differences. The words are highlighted with different colors to indicate similarities.

5. Remind the children to use their knowledge of letter–sound relationships to read new words (Taberski, 2000, p. 93). This critical step encourages transfer of skills from one context to another. Students must be asked to demonstrate the use of their new skill in their own reading or, as Taberski says, "All the work we do together looking for spelling patterns and listening to sounds is of little use if they don't apply it as they read" (p. 93).

Some teachers might be concerned that because of the multiple rereadings of the text, the children are simply memorizing the words and are not truly reading them. Vacca et al. (2003) address this concern: "Imitation establishes good models. The reading-like behaviors associated with an imitative stage of reading provide children with important early book experiences" (p. 87).

For younger readers, shared reading is often done with an enlarged text such as a poetry chart or Big Book, which is literally a giant-size version of a children's book. A Big Book allows a large group of students to see the pictures and the text so that the teacher can involve them in learning activities.

An incredible variety of Big Books is now available, including poetry and nonfiction texts. They often feature rhythmic language, rhyme, repetition, or refrains. They also tend to be predictable; that is, the author provides enough clues so that even the youngest student can predict what will happen next, which promotes interest and comprehension. Figure 5.1 lists Big Books that emphasize rhythm, rhyme, repetition, and prediction.

Shared reading can continue into the middle grades and beyond. Allen (2000) reports that middle and high school students make significant gains in reading when they read a text silently as it is read aloud by a fluent reader. Rycik and Irvin (2005) suggest that students might be given a selected passage from a text that their teacher has read aloud in order to read it intensively in a small group. Students might, for example, search out unfamiliar words and work together to identify them by using both sound and sense cues. The teacher might also delete selected words or parts of words in much the same way as Ms. Kelly.

■ FIGURE 5.1   Big Books that Emphasize Rhythm, Rhyme, Repetition, and Prediction

Brown Bear, Brown Bear What Do You See? Martin, B. (1983). New York: Rinehart-Winston.

Bunny Hop. Nesheim, L. (1995). Bothwell, WA: Wright Group.

Caps for Sale. Slobodkina, E. (1996). New York: Harper Collins.

The Cats of Tiffany Street. Hayes, S. (1996). Boston: Houghton Mifflin.

Down by the Bay. Daniel, A. (1992). Bothwell, WA: Wright Group.

Elephants Aloft. Appelt, K. (1993). San Diego: Hartcourt Brace.

Father's Old Gray Whiskers. Daniel, A. (1993). Bothwell, WA: Wright Group.

Flower Garden. Bunting, E. (1994). New York: Scholastic.

Frog on a Log. Genter, N. (1995). Bothwell, WA: Wright Group.

In the Tall, Tall Grass. Fleming, D. (1993). New York: Henry Holt.

The Jacket I Wear in the Snow. Neitzel, S. (1997). New York: Mulberry Big Books.

Jamberry. Degen, B. (1983). New York: Harper & Row.

King Bidgood's in the Bathtub. Wood, A. (1985). San Diego: Hartcourt Brace.

The Little Red Hen. Barton, B. (1994). New York: Harper & Row.

Mama Zooms. Cowen-Fletcher, J. (1993). New York: Scholastic.

Mouse Paint. Walsh, E. (1989). San Diego: Hartcourt Brace.

Mrs. Wishy-Washy. Cowley, J. (1999). New York: Philomel Books.

The Napping House. Wood, A. (1994). San Diego: Hartcourt Brace.

Over in the Meadow. Daniel, A. (1995). Bothwell, WA: Wright Group.

USING POETRY AND VERSE

Poetry and rhyme may be the perfect context for teaching phonics skills. The short text of a poem can be read and enjoyed by the students during one lesson and then reread several times to make discoveries about the words within the poem. Many teachers write poems on large chart paper and laminate them so that they can be used year after year, and students can use a transparency pen to circle elements in the poem. Rasinski and Padak (2001) also recommend making smaller copies of the poem so that each student can have an individual copy of it to read independently.

Maurice Sendak's popular book of poems, *Chicken Soup with Rice* (1962), is an excellent source of poems that can be enjoyed each month of the year and also can be used to teach common rime patterns. Take a look at the poem "January" and find the rime pattern:

> *In January*
> *It's so nice*
> *While slipping*

On the sliding ice
To sip hot chicken soup
With rice.
Sipping once
Sipping twice
Sipping chicken soup
With rice.

Clearly, the *-ice* pattern is prominent in this poem. The words *nice, ice, rice,* and *twice* should be identified by the children. One interesting way to do this is to take a plastic flyswatter and cut a rectangular shaped hole in the center. The students then use this to "capture" the rime chunks in the poem. The words with the rime should be written on chart paper. The teacher and students can then generate a list of other words that have the same pattern, such as *dice, lice, price, slice, spice,* and *advice,* which can be added to the list. This chart can then be used to help write a group poem written by the class or individual poems written by the students. For example, the class might write their own poem called:

Advice to Mice

Think twice
Little mice
Before you take a slice
We don't think
That's very nice.

Naturally, all poems should be displayed, read enthusiastically aloud, and brought home to share with parents. Many teachers have their students keep poetry notebooks in which they keep copies of all of the chart poems they have read in class, as well as any student-generated ones. Once students have used rime patterns in this meaningful way, they become attuned to noticing them in other contexts and using them correctly in their own writing. This same procedure can be used with other poems. A survey of the poems in *Chicken Soup with Rice* reveals the rime patterns *-oor, -ay, -est, -oop, -eep, -eap, -ot, -ile, -ost, -ale,* and *-ail* used in various poems.

POETRY AND RHYME IN INTERMEDIATE AND MIDDLE GRADES   Poetry can also be a great way to teach word identification with older students. The short text allows for in-depth, concentrated word analysis. Poems that have rhyming texts can give valuable cues to pronunciation. For example, in the poem "The Weevils" by Douglas Florian (1998), the word *evil* is quite helpful in pronouncing the words *weevil, primeval,* and *medieval.*

The Weevils

We are weevils.
We are evil

We've aggrieved
Since time primeval.
With our down-curved
Beaks we bore.
Into crops
And trees we gore.
We are ruinous.
We are rotten.
We drill holes
Into bolls of cotton.
We're not modern,
We're medieval.
We are weevils
We are evil.

In addition to graphophonemic cues, the author provides enough semantic and syntactical cues in the poem to help students figure out the meaning of *aggrieved, bore, gore, ruinous, bolls,* and *medieval.*

HINK PINKS   Students in intermediate and middle grades enjoy creating **hink pinks,** a pair of rhyming words that serve as the answer to a riddle. Hink pinks are most easily created by working backwards, by first selecting a pair of rhyming words that will be the answer to the riddle. For instance, a student might choose the words *nice ice* and then write the riddle: "What do rappers call their jewelry?" Hink pinks can also be multisyllable (hinky pinkies): Where do inflatables go swimming? (the balloon lagoon).

☐ TEACHING AND LEARNING WITH DECODABLE TEXT

Decodable texts employ words that are primarily phonetically regular. They are often produced in a series in which the first book might emphasize a certain letter sound (such as short /e/) and later books would gradually add other sound elements. Advocates sometimes argue that decodable texts allow young children to begin applying their decoding skills to books very early in their schooling. However, decodable texts often seem to sacrifice meaning for decoding in sentences such as "The bug digs up the rug." As Graves, Juel, and Graves (1998) observe: "The text has a tongue-twisty feel and certainly does not demonstrate a natural use of language. . . . The approach seriously constrains the content and the story" (p. 148).

No research has found that the use of decodable text is a superior overall method for teaching reading to beginning readers (Cunningham, 2000). Mesmer (2001), however, reviewed the research on decodable text and concluded that it can be useful with children who are making the transition from the partial alphabetic stage (Ehri, 1998) to the full alphabetic stage where they are able to use phonetic patterns in words to assist their reading.

Brown (1999/2000) also argued that there is a place for decodable text within a primary classroom. She suggested that different kinds of texts could be used to scaffold instruction for students at different developmental levels. She concluded that decodable texts are most useful for students who need help "breaking the code" and making the bridge between "learning about print and being fluent with print" (p. 299).

The challenge for teachers is to seek out well-written decodable texts that provide students with a sense of accomplishment after they have read the book independently. Fortunately, several such books have appeared on the market. *I Like Mess* (Leonard, 1998) is a charming book with photographs of a real little girl named Tess who indeed likes to make a mess. Beginning readers can easily use graphophonemic and picture cues to read sentences such as "This makes Mom sad" and "This makes Dad mad." The book has an authentic ending in which Tess cleans up her mess and then makes another one.

Mouse Makes Words (Helig & Hembrook, 2002) demonstrates in a comical way how to use onsets and rimes to create new words. For example, mouse finds the word *hat*, then takes off the *h*, carts in a *c*, "Yikes! Now it is CAT!" Most of these newer books combine easily decodable words with high frequency words to make them more readable. Usborne Publishing has a series of simple texts that are labeled "Easy words to read" at the top and "A phonics reader" at the bottom.

Many of these books include a kind of teacher's guide that shows the word patterns featured in the book and some teaching suggestions. Scholastic publishes a set of phonics chapter books with longer texts on each page and stories that could actually be discussed.

There are indications that decodable text has a role to play in an overall literacy program, as long as it is not a major focus for instruction. Some guidelines for using decodable text in the classroom appear in Figure 5.2.

Perhaps the best way to use simple, easily decodable text in the classroom is for teachers and students to create their own. For example, a group of pre-service teachers created this story to emphasize the -*ack* and -*ap* rime chunks:

A boy named **Jack** wore a **black backpack** with a **flap** that had a **snap.** Inside the **flap** there was a **map.** The **map** led him to a **stack** of CDs. To his surprise it was a **trap** guarded by a giant rat. While the rat took a **nap,** Jack ran away as if he was in a race on a **track.**

Although it certainly will not be mistaken for great literature, this story has meaning and is fun and appealing to students. More importantly, beginning readers should be able to read it independently while practicing the familiar spelling patterns.

■ FIGURE 5.2   Guidelines for Using Decodable Texts

- Decodable text should never be the only instructional text. It should be regarded as supplemental to a reading program.
- The most effective use of decodable text is by students during independent reading to reinforce instruction in phonetic patterns.
- Only use decodable text that has an identifiable plot and can be discussed with students.
- Look for newer decodable texts that emphasize rhyming and decoding by analogy, rather than letter-by-letter decoding.
- Have children notice high frequency words in the text that are not phonetically regular (such as *said* or *was*) and help them to realize that decoding is not the only way to figure out words and that they must use other strategies too.

☐ GUIDED READING USING LEVELED TEXTS

Guided reading involves working with students in small groups to develop reading strategies that will enable the students to read increasingly more difficult texts. Crucial to the implementation of guided reading is selecting books on the appropriate developmental level of the students: not easy enough for the student to read independently, but not so difficult that the student struggles over every word. This is done through the use of **leveled texts,** books that have been identified as being on a particular developmental reading level. Fountas and Pinnell (1996) have developed a widely used leveling system that classifies books from level A (beginning kindergarten) to Z (end of sixth grade).

The goal of guided reading according to Fountas and Pinnell (1996) is to help students develop a repertoire of problem-solving strategies that they can apply in any reading situation. One essential problem-solving strategy is using phonics to help identify words. At the start of a guided reading lesson, the teacher does a book introduction designed to support students so that they will be able to read the book independently. The book introduction is tailored to the developmental reading level of the students and to the particular features of the book.

Emergent and beginning readers require a more extensive book introduction, often involving a "picture walk" through the book with the teacher asking the students to notice what is happening throughout the book. At this opportunity, the teacher is able to introduce new and challenging words such as proper names, but also can remind students how to use the compare–contrast strategy to read new words with the same spelling pattern. Older, more proficient readers will need only a brief, focused book introduction before reading, but may also have their attention drawn to individual words and word analysis.

Fountas and Pinnell (1996) caution that regardless of reading level, students must be given the chance to use their problem-solving strategies. The initial coaching during the book introduction encourages students to use these strategies while they read on their own. Figures 5.3 and 5.4 show examples of guided reading book introductions on the primary- and middle-grade levels.

■ FIGURE 5.3   Guided Reading Book Introduction: Primary Level

Text: *Henry and Mudge in the Sparkle Days* by Cynthia Rylant
Fountas and Pinnell Level J (Grade 2), a simple chapter book

1. Mr. Taylor tells the students that all the stories in this book have something in common. He asks them to look at the picture on the cover and try to figure out what it is. (The cover shows a boy and a dog playing in the snow.) The children conclude that all the stories take place in winter.

2. Mr. Taylor has decided that two of the words from the story are important to the meaning and provide practice in using word-solving strategies, so he asks the students to figure out the word *sparkle* by looking on the word wall and comparing it to the key word *shark*. He has them use compare/contrast to decode the word *creature* by comparing it with the known words *beat* and *picture*.

3. Mr. Taylor asks the children to speculate why the author named the book *In the Sparkle Days,* and they respond by demonstrating their background knowledge of how snow sparkles in the wintertime. Mr. Taylor has them read the titles of the stories in the table of contents, and after reading "Christmas Eve Dinner," Brian says that ornaments on his Christmas tree sparkle too; and when the students turn the pages of the story "Firelight," they notice that there are many kinds of light illustrated—lights inside houses, stars, moonlight, and a fire in the fireplace.

4. Mr. Taylor asks the students to turn to page 16 in their books. On this page Mudge the dog is digging a hole in the snow with his nose. Underneath is the passage, "He used his nose to dig a little hole. *Ah-choo!* went Mudge. Snow always made him sneeze." Mr. Taylor took the role of a student trying to figure out the word *Ah-choo.* "I'm not sure what that word is. I think I'll read past it and see if the rest of the sentence helps. Oh, snow makes Mudge sneeze. Maybe that word has something to do with sneezing. That part *choo* looks like *boo.* I know. That word is *ah-choo,* the sound we make when we sneeze. When you read and are stuck on a word, skip it and read on and ask what word would make sense, then go back and see if the letters in the word fit that word."

5. Mr. Taylor asks the students if they are happy when the first snowfall comes. After a short discussion of the good and bad things about snow, Mr. Taylor asks the students to read the first story in the book and find out if Henry and Mudge enjoy the first snowfall and why. He also reminds the students to use the "skip and return" method if they get stuck on a word.

Text: *Buried in Ice* (nonfiction) by Owen Beatie and John Geiger
Fountas and Pinnell Level W (Grade 6)

Students need to see that nonfiction has a different structure than fiction and often requires different strategies to read it. *Buried in Ice* has some helpful features such as clear, full-color illustrations, a glossary of terms (but no pronunciations), maps, and actual photographs of artifacts from a doomed Arctic expedition that attempted to find the Northwest Passage in 1845. The text also has some difficult features: the book has an unusual format that switches from present to past and from different points of view; there is dialogue included that gives a fictional aspect to factual events; and there are some difficult words and proper names that students may have trouble reading.

Mrs. Sanchez has chosen to deal with the format first.

1. Mrs. Sanchez asks the students to turn to the table of contents and notice that there are seven chapters in the book. She also briefly explains the purpose of an epilogue. The students turn to the first chapter and Mrs. Sanchez reads the first sentence. "I can see the graves! I shouted to the pilot of the Twin Otter as we approached Beechey Island." She elicits from the students that this chapter is written in first person and explains that one of the authors of the book (Beattie) is an anthropologist (defined in the glossary) who is writing this book about his scientific discoveries during an expedition to the Arctic by Sir John Franklin and his men. Mrs. Sanchez has the students turn to Chapters 6 and 7 and determine that these chapters are written in the present. She then contrasts these chapters with Chapters 3, 4, and 5, which are written through the point of view of Luke, a young stoker on board the ship *H.M.S. Terror.*

2. Mrs. Sanchez then turns her attention to the words in the text. She realizes that some words are easy for the students to decode but may have meanings unknown to them. She demonstrates this with the word *stoker* and directs students to find it in the glossary. Next, Mrs. Sanchez turns attention to multisyllable words that students may have trouble pronouncing. She shows students how to "chunk" parts of a long word into manageable parts, such as *tu-ber-cu-los-is.* She does this for proper names as well, such as In-u-it. Mrs. Sanchez also has students notice that prefixes and suffixes can give clues to meaning such as in *anthropologist* and *tripod.* Mrs. Sanchez gives each student in the group a pack of sticky notes and asks them to mark any words that they have trouble with and cannot find in the glossary. She tells them that they will compare lists tomorrow, but she does not want them to interrupt their reading to look up words in the dictionary now.

3. Before dismissing the group to begin reading Chapter 1, Mrs. Sanchez reminds students that the job of the scientist is to make conclusions based on facts, and that while they are reading, they should keep a list of the conclusions Beattie made about the Franklin expedition and what facts support these conclusions.

☐ TEACHING WORD IDENTIFICATION IN LITERAT

Literature circles are small heterogeneous groups of students who together to discuss a book that they have all read. According to D: (2002), who first developed this approach, it is essential that the stu: choose their own reading materials, that the groups are temporary but on a regular schedule while reading a book, and that the discussion is led by students. The teacher acts as a facilitator, not a group member.

Students may use "role sheets" developed by Daniels (2002) to take on specific responsibilities within the group such as "Summarizer," "Questioner," or "Researcher." Two of these roles focus on close inspection of words: "Word Wizard" (for fiction) and "Vocabulary Enricher" (for nonfiction). The responsibility for both of these roles is to record words that are puzzling, unfamiliar, interesting, or unusual in some way. Students with these roles write down the word and page number, find the definition from the dictionary or other source, and then plan for a discussion of the words.

A GLIMPSE INTO A GRADE 5/6 CLASSROOM: MRS. LANYI

Mrs. Lanyi has been using literature circles to teach reading for quite a few years. She used the role sheets "ages ago" but found that they restricted students' discussions and sometimes prevented them from focusing on the text as a whole. Her current students use reading logs instead of role sheets as a way of preparing for their group meetings.

On the afternoon we visit Mrs. Lanyi's class, two groups of students are scattered around the large, comfortable room working in their reading logs. The students have been instructed to write anything that would promote discussion and help the group discover the "big ideas." Their log entries can include questions, predictions, inferences, memorable quotes from the book, or "sketch to stretch" illustrations that show important ideas.

Mrs. Lanyi always encourages the students to record vocabulary words in their reading logs and then to look them up in the dictionary. We observe one boy who is working at a round table looking up the word *bamboozled* in the dictionary. He is unable to find it, but works out the pronunciation by chunking it into parts. He reads the sentence in which the word was used and concludes that it means "to fool someone." He then records this information in his log.

Meanwhile, two other groups meet to discuss their books: *A Gathering of Days* (Blos, 1979) and *Steal Away Home* (Ruby, 1994). The two literature circles are having lively discussions. A reading teacher and a tutor sit in with the groups to facilitate discussion, but the students do the majority of the talking. The teachers occasionally move the discussion along by asking questions such as "Why do you think so?" or "Where's your evidence?"

Because the groups are heterogeneous and multiage, some students are more fluent than others, but they serve as role models for the younger, less proficient readers. Every student is expected to participate fully. At the end of the discussion, the students do both self-evaluations and peer evaluations by using a rubric in their reading logs. It spells out expectations for a grade based on their preparation and discussion that day.

To get an A, students must "extend" the discussion; a B indicates that they "generate" discussion. The students not only discuss the story with a high level of sophistication, but also show maturity in their evaluations. One student, for example, tells another student, "My opinion is that you deserve at least a B because you made connections that helped you understand the story."

After her circle is finished, a girl named Sabrina shares her reading log. She proudly explains how she got an A for the day because she had made the extra effort to look up the word *cipher* online after finding that it was not in the dictionary.

Sabrina explains that her book *Gathering of Days* (Blos, 1979) is a diary of a girl set in colonial times, so "they talk very different." To illustrate this point, Sabrina reads a passage from the book: "It requires but little discernment to discover the imperfections of others; but much humility to acknowledge our own" (p. 31).

When asked how she figured out these difficult words and their meanings, Sabrina replies that she "whisper reads" a hard passage several times and tries to sound out the words. Then she writes it in her log. Sabrina also points out another sentence that is a note written by a homeless man: "Pleeze miss. Take pitty. I am cold" (Blos, p. 20). Sabrina comments, "You can tell that he's not educated."

Like other teachers who use literature circles, Mrs. Lanyi frequently conducts whole class or small group mini lessons on various aspects of reading. These include lessons in which she uses picture books to teach strategies for identifying multisyllable words. The students in Mrs. Lanyi's classroom have learned the importance of words: how to read and understand them, how to use them effectively in their discussions of literature, and how authors purposefully choose words to convey meaning.

INTERVENTIONS WHEN STUDENTS STRUGGLE

Children with intelligent quotients of 85 or below are considered to have intelligence developmental delays and may qualify for special education. They may find reading to be a difficult task. Research reported by Polloway, Miller, and Smith (2004), however, shows that a large proportion of children in special education programs, who are at risk for reading failure, can be helped to learn if the proper interventions are given. Read how Krista Alberty engages her students in working with words.

A Glimpse into the Classroom: Mrs. Alberty

We observe Mrs. Alberty as she welcomes four boys into her intervention classroom and asks them to sit around a table. She directs their attention to the first word in the title of a new picture book she is holding. "Look at the first word. What word is that? It's a number word. It goes with our story today."

One student responds, "One," and Mrs. Alberty praises him. As she passes out the simple patterned books, Mrs. Alberty reinforces the title by saying, "One for you, and one for me. Every time you see this word, it's going to be the same. What do you think this book could be about?"

The boys look at the picture on the cover and notice a child dividing up his food. Mrs. Alberty and her students then do a shared reading of the book in unison. She subtly "fades out" from time to time and lets the boys take over. When they get stuck on a word, she helps them to use all cueing systems. For example, when one boy struggles with the word *bite,* she asks him to look at the first letter and make the /b/ sound. She then directs him to look at the picture of the boy fishing. When the child guesses the word *candy,* she asks him, "Would you feed candy to a fish? Does that make sense?"

Throughout the lesson, Mrs. Alberty offers gentle correction and positive feedback to her students. She praises all of their efforts to read independently, and challenges them to explain their thinking by asking questions like, "How did you figure that out?"

☐ Assessing Word Identification with Meaningful Texts

Assessing the way students identify words can be done using the same literature you use for instruction. Clay (2000) developed **running records,** a systematic method for observing and recording how young students monitor their own reading. The teacher keeps a graphic record of the child's reading, usually on a blank piece of paper, using a shorthand code; for example, a check mark indicates a correct word. When a child substitutes a word that is different from the text, it is written above that word.

An omission from the text is recorded as a dash above the word, and an insertion is a dash below the word. The repetition of a single word is marked with an *R;* the repetition of a whole phrase is shown with an arrow. If a child self-corrects a word, it is marked *SC,* and if a teacher must intervene and supply a word, it is marked with a *T.*

After the reading is recorded, the teacher analyzes the miscues made by the student to check for a pattern of errors that would indicate overreliance on one particular cueing system. Look at the following examples.

1. If a child consistently makes miscues that look similar to the word in the text but does not mean the same, such as *horse* for *house,* then the child is relying primarily on visual cues. This student tries to "sound out" a word he does not know and will often substitute a nonsense word.

2. If a child consistently makes miscues that have the same meaning as the words in the text but do not fit the sound–symbol pattern, such as *pony* for *horse,* then she is relying primarily on meaning cues. This student pays attention to the meaning of the text, but is not being careful enough about matching letters to sounds.

3. If a child consistently makes miscues that "sound right" in the sentence (fits the syntax) and is the same part of speech as the word in the text, such as *jumped* for *walked,* then he is using structure cues. This student usually is also paying some attention to the meaning of the text because his miscues sound right in the structure of the sentence, but the meaning may also be changed.

Students need to balance the three cueing systems to construct meaning from a text. If students rely too much on one cue, then they fail to use all the resources available to them to unlock new words. The teacher's job is to identify which cueing systems are lacking and teach each student how to use all three.

A teacher can also gain a great deal of insight from looking closely at what a student does when faced with an unknown word. Does the student consistently attempt to figure out the word? This indicates a student who is a "risk-taker" and should be praised for the effort even if unsuccessful. Conversely, a student who is silent and consistently looks to the teacher for help may lack word identification strategies that are needed to become an independent reader.

Running records are most appropriate for assessing primary students' reading. Older students may benefit from an **informal reading inventory (IRI),** consisting of reading passages written at increasingly higher grade levels. Usually both fiction and nonfiction passages are included, with comprehension questions for each passage. The student reads from one copy of the passage, and the teacher has a separate copy on which to mark miscues. By combining information about the number and kind of miscues a student makes and the number of questions the student answers correctly, the teacher can estimate the student's reading level.

Teachers can also assess many of the key elements of cue usage by listening to students reading a page or two from the books they are reading in class. The teacher should listen for indications of effective cue use such as the following:

- The words that were read were real words.
- The words that were read fit the syntax of the sentence.
- The words that were read fit the sense of the sentence.
- The words that were read fit the letters and sounds.

- Miscues were self-corrected.
- The reading was easy and fluent.

After listening to the reading, the teacher can mark a simple checklist of these items with *A* for always, *S* for sometimes, or *NO* for not observed. Teachers should try to follow up on individual assessments of cue usage with a conference in which they and the students discuss the meaning of the assessment and collaborate to set goals for improvement if needed.

▫   ▫   ▫   ▫   ▫

BEFORE YOU MOVE ON

Check Your Understanding

Write five "possible sentences" about the ideas in this chapter by combining two or more of the following words and phrases in each sentence.

Big Books	Leveled Texts	Literature Circles
embedded instruction	meaningful context	running records
shared reading	planning for spontaneity	decodable text
authentic assessment	poetry and verse	guided reading

Now combine your sentences into your own chapter summary.

WHAT'S IN THIS CHAPTER FOR ME?

Early Childhood Teachers

By reading the opening scenario, you have a good idea of how phonics and word identification can be taught using children's literature. Using Big Books and poetry in a shared reading format is an excellent way to teach primary students. Check out some of the books in Figure 5.1 to use with students. Be sure to read the guidelines for using decodable text wisely in Figure 5.2, and read carefully how to do a book introduction in guided reading. You may soon be doing this yourself. Read carefully the section on assessing word identification through running records. This practice is common in primary schools and will be of great benefit to you.

Middle Grade Teachers

Be sure to read carefully the description of how Mrs. Lanyi conducts literature circles in her grade 5/6 classroom. This is an excellent model for embedding skills instruction within a meaningful literature context. Poetry should also be part of your teaching, and using interesting poems such as *The Weevils* and fun verse with hink pinks can motivate middle grade students. Be sure to read the book introduction for middle grades. This is a good model for teaching skills with literature. Read the section about assessing word identification. Informal reading inventories have graded reading passages up to eighth grade, or beyond, that can be used to assess students' word identification, comprehension, and fluency with both fiction and nonfiction texts.

Intervention Specialists

By reading the opening scenario, you have a good idea of how phonics and word identification can be taught using children's literature. Using Big Books and poetry in a shared reading format is an excellent way to teach all students, including those with special needs. Using decodable text can also work well with struggling readers, although it should never be used exclusively. Check out some of the books in Figure 5.1 to share with students. Read the guidelines in Figure 5.2.

Carefully read the discussion about intervention with delayed readers and note how Krista Alberty uses meaningful texts to teach word identification to her students. Finally, read carefully the section on assessing reading with running records and informal reading inventories. As an intervention specialist, an important part of your job is identifying appropriate goals for students, and these assessments can help you to do this.

SPELLING AND WRITING INSTRUCTION

I t is writing workshop time in Mr. Allen's fifth-grade classroom. Paul and Kwan huddle in a corner of their classroom reading each other's story drafts. Their job is to edit their partner's work.

"The spell-check said I spelled *separate* wrong. No way, man, it sounds like *sep- er- ate* and that's what I put."

"That may be the way you say it, but it's not the way you write it. English sucks, man. I'm trying to figure out which word to use in this sentence, '*They're going to my game on Saturday.*' I don't know which *there* to use. They all sound the same."

"I guess since it's your game, then it's the one that means you own something. I don't know for sure though. Ask Mr. Allen."

If you were Mr. Allen, what would you say to Paul and Kwan? How would you explain words that are not always spelled the way that they sound and how would you teach words that sound the same but are spelled differently?

Consider the following questions before you continue reading:

- Do writers use the same decoding processes as readers?
- Why are some people better spellers than others?
- How do teachers teach students spelling while teaching writing?

Although phonics can be an effective strategy for teaching spelling, it is not the only strategy you will use to help students with their spelling and writing. As students progress through different stages of spelling development, there are a number of clever and useful classroom activities that allow you to teach spelling while you help students to improve their writing.

ORTHOGRAPHY: A LANGUAGE FOR SPELLERS

Orthography refers to how graphemes are arranged into identifiable patterns in a language, in other words, spelling. When students have **orthographic knowledge,** they recognize familiar spelling patterns. For example, Paul and Kwan would probably have no trouble reading the nonsense word *jark* because they are familiar with the -*ark* spelling pattern; however, they would be confounded if they tried to read *xzelw,* because the spelling, the orthography, looks strange. Paul and Kwan struggle with the peculiarities of English orthography. Kwan, as a second language learner, is trying to learn English and adapt to a new and different orthography. Paul and Kwan recognize that a knowledge of phonics will only get them so far. They need to combine this knowledge with visual memorization of some sight words in order to be good spellers.

HIGH FREQUENCY WORDS

The most common words in the English language are called **high frequency words,** or **sight words.** Students should not spend time stopping to decode these words; they should recognize them by sight. Unfortunately, many of these words are particularly troublesome for students for several reasons. First, some high frequency words are phonetically irregular. Words such as *said, some, have,* and *what* do not follow the phonic rules for vowel phonemes. Second, many high frequency words are abstract and serve only as **function words** within the context of a sentence. You cannot easily explain the meaning of such words as *of, the,* or *was* but only demonstrate their use in a sentence. Finally, many high frequency words look similar. For example,

■ FIGURE 6.1   Sight Word Resources

The two most used lists of sight words are the Dolch list and the Fry list. Both contain words culled from the most common words to occur in beginning reading texts. The Dolch word list is divided into grade levels, whereas the Fry list consists of 300 "instant words."

There are many websites that contain these word lists as well as suggestions on how to use them. To find the most current, do a keyword search on *sight words.* Following are some of the more interesting sites.

createdbyteachers.com/sightfreemain.html has lists of Dolch words by grade level and handy checklists for assessment of these words.

gate.net/~labooks/XLPDolch.html features fable stories to practice reading Dolch words in context. There are also lesson plans, puzzles, and activities using Dolch words.

On teachers.net, you can find teacher-created games using Dolch words.

usu.edu/teachall/text/reading/Frylist.df features the 300 Fry words; and *flashcardexchange.com* allows you to export any Fry words and turn them into flashcards.

when, where, what, want, and *were* begin with *w* and have similar **visual configurations.**

Take a look at the following words and sort them into two groups: ones that would be easy for a beginner reader to read and spell and ones that would be difficult to read and spell.

and	said	now	their	when
the	come	bring	one	cold
know	eight	orange	does	sleep

An important characteristic of a fluent reader is the ability to recall high frequency words with **automaticity,** that is, effortlessly and fluently. If students stop to decode too many words, they often lose focus and may not adequately comprehend the text. Therefore, it is imperative that high frequency words be systematically taught. Figure 6.1 contains internet resources for lists of high frequency words and ideas for teaching them. It is important that students learn to both read and spell high frequency words. Teachers need to have a knowledge of developmental spelling stages to help their students do this.

☐ DEVELOPMENTAL SPELLING STAGES

Researchers (Gentry, 2002; Bear et al., 2000; Pinnell & Fountas, 1998; Calfee, 1998; Treiman, 1998; Henderson, 1990) have determined that children progress through developmental stages of spelling. The following is a synthesis of the stages these researchers have identified.

☐ PREPHONEMIC STAGE

At the earliest stage of the prephonemic spelling level, students do not associate letters with a particular sound. The first written word a child is likely to learn to spell is his or her name. Typically, children use the letters in their names to attempt to write other words. This indicates that they realize that speech can be represented by written symbols even if there is a lack of awareness that certain letters represent certain sounds.

In the later part of this stage, students begin to use initial consonants to represent a word. For example, *B* might be used to indicate *bear* or *Beth*. Near the end of this stage, students begin to use beginning and ending consonants to spell words. Take a look at Alex's writing in Figure 6.2. At the time that this was written, Alex was 5 years old and in a prekindergarten class. He had been taught letter names and had begun to associate some letters with sounds. Notice how Alex repeats the letters in his name, and ones that have similar shapes, such as *H* and *A*. Alex also explained that several of the other letters represent the first letter in the names of his friends. Can you see how Alex spelled *Quinn, Jacob*, and *Zach*? Alex does not yet have a concept of words being separated by spaces, but he has a beginning understanding of how sounds can be represented by letters. Therefore, Alex is in the prephonemic spelling stage.

PHONEMIC STAGE

When children enter the phonemic stage of spelling, they make a very important addition to their writing: vowels. Students associate letters with sounds and will attempt to sound out a word in order to spell it. The words produced often have a one-to-one correspondence between letters and

■ **FIGURE 6.2** Alex's Writing

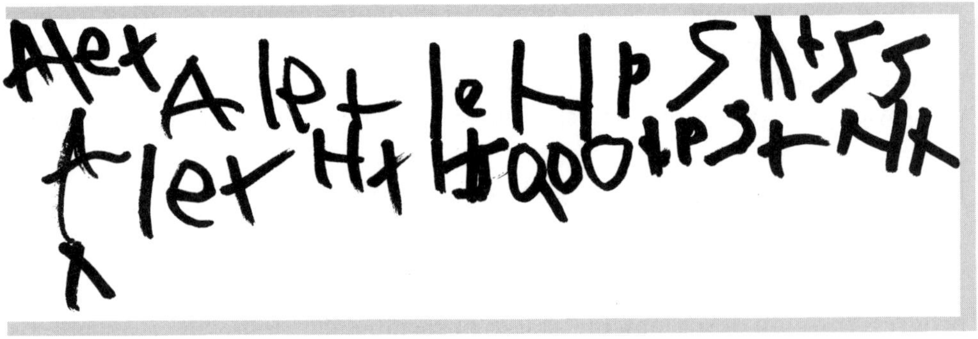

sounds, but not necessarily an awareness of spelling patterns such as the CVCe pattern. For example, a child at this stage might spell *boat* as *b-o-t.* Look at Katie's writing in Figure 6.3. Katie is the authors' daughter. Her first-grade teacher kept a portfolio of all students' writing to document their growth over time. You can see her progress through the spelling stages. In October, Katie wrote *lik* to represent *like,* showing a 1:1 correspondence and lack of understanding of silent letters. Although she knew that *k* can represent the /k/ sound, she was unaware that *y* is used to make the /i/ sound in *my.* Katie made a good attempt to sound out the word *guinea* in *guinea pig.* At this developmental stage, Katie is a phonemic speller.

■ **FIGURE 6.3   Katie's Writing (October)**

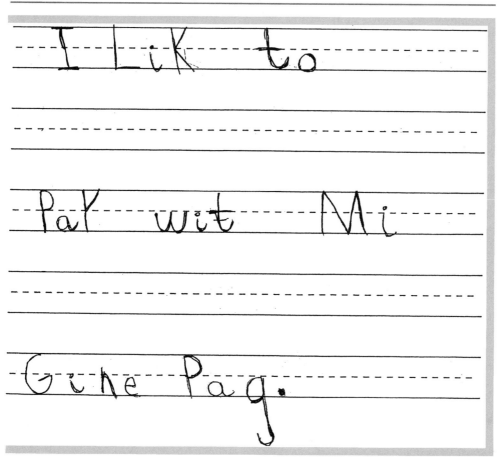

TRANSITIONAL STAGE

Now compare Katie's writing in January in Figure 6.4 with that from October. What do you notice? Katie demonstrates an orthographic awareness of spelling patterns. Students at this level may still show an awareness of spelling patterns without choosing the right one. For example, a student may spell *keep* as *cepe*, showing an understanding that /k/ can be spelled two different ways, and that a CVVC and a CVCe pattern can both produce a long vowel sound. Likewise, *hope* could be spelled *hoap* if the student compared it to the spelling of *soap*. Katie also demonstrates an ability to spell several high frequency words such as *like, my, it,* and *is*. It is possible that she copied the spelling of *animal* from a source in the room, a behavior that should be encouraged rather than discouraged.

CONVENTIONAL STAGE

By about third grade, most students have developed an orthographic awareness to the point that they can spell most high frequency words that conform to phonic rules, such as *his*, and many that do not conform, such as

■ **FIGURE 6.4   Katie's Writing (January)**

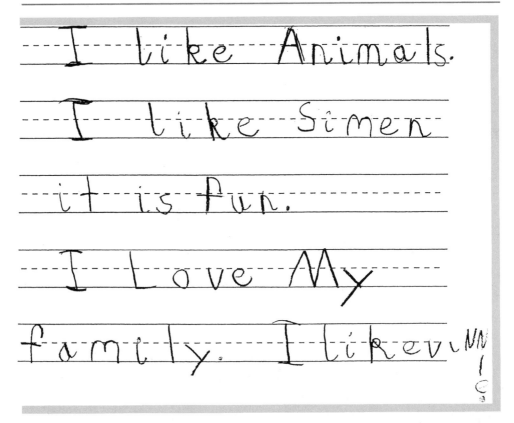

■ **FIGURE 6.5**   Katie's Second-Grade Writing

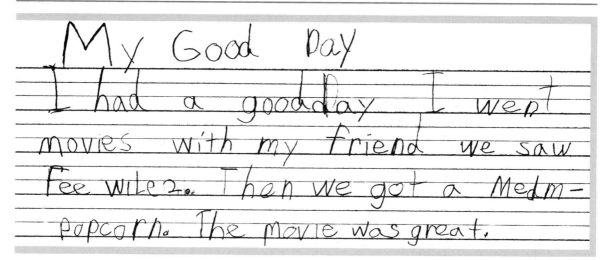

said. They have had enough repeated practice with common spelling patterns that they can anticipate many word spellings. Look at Katie's writing in second grade in Figure 6.5. She is beginning to show command over high frequency words and successfully wrote the phonetically irregular word *great*. It is important to note that students at this stage attempt to spell longer and more difficult words such as Katie did with *medium*. Children should be encouraged to do this to make their writing more interesting. Otherwise, they will tend to stick with safer, easier words such as *big*.

The following table is a summary of the basic developmental stages of spelling.

DEVELOPMENTAL SPELLING STAGES	
STAGE	**SPELLING BEHAVIORS**
Prephonemic	■ Uses letters in his/her name ■ Does not usually associate letters with sounds ■ May use beginning consonants to represent whole words (e.g., *B* = *bear*)
Phonemic	■ Writes one letter to represent each sound (e.g., *bot* = *boat*) ■ Uses vowels, but not in spelling patterns like silent *e*
Transitional	Shows awareness of spelling patterns, but not always the correct ones (e.g., *hoap* = *hope*)
Conventional	Can spell most phonetically regular words correctly, but not all words encountered

■ FIGURE 6.6   Spelling Counts!

A would-be robber in Gainesville, Florida, recently discovered that spelling really does matter. In his note to the bank teller, he wrote, "If a die pack blows, so do you," confusing the word *die* with *dye*. The same wording was used in two other robberies making it easy to tie all the crimes to the same suspect. Police Sergeant Keith Kameg was quoted as remarking, "If anything says education is important to your future, this case says that . . . . As simple as spelling one word wrong was instrumental in solving three bank robberies."

Source: Spelling Counts, (2004, February 20). The *Akron Beacon Journal.*

☐ INVENTED SPELLING

In recent years, it has become popular to use the term **invented spelling** to refer to the kind of writing that students do in the phonemic and transitional stages of spelling development. Unfortunately, this term has been widely misinterpreted. The intent is to encourage students to listen to the sounds they hear in words and to try and translate those sounds into their corresponding letters. We want students to take the risk in trying to spell words themselves instead of relying on the teacher to always supply the correct spelling. However, the term *invented spelling* seems to imply that any spelling is acceptable and that kids should be encouraged to "be creative" in their writing and not worry about conforming to any standards. Many parents have interpreted invented spelling in this way and have seen it as a sign of lack of rigor in American schools. Try to avoid using the term *invented spelling;* instead refer to it as **phonetic** or **temporary spelling,** which better reflects the developmental nature of spelling. Parents need to hear the message that teachers fully expect students to progress toward conventional spelling, and that it is the teachers' job to help students move through these stages. Read the newspaper article in Figure 6.6 to see the consequences of not learning conventional spelling.

☐ GUIDING PRINCIPLES FOR SPELLING INSTRUCTION

Researchers have found that spelling needs to be actively taught and not left to chance (Gentry, 2002; Bear et al., 2000; Pinnell & Fountas, 1998, Calfee, 1998; Treiman, 1998). Nonetheless, most researchers believe that spelling should be incorporated as part of reading and writing instruction rather than taught as a separate subject. The following are guiding principles for spelling instruction.

- "Look for what students use but confuse" (Routman, 2000). By studying students' patterns of spelling errors, teachers can plan future instruction. For example, if you notice that your students often misspell *r*-controlled words in their writing, plan a lesson on how to hear the differences.

- Focus first on the spelling of high frequency words and stress automaticity. Insist that students use word walls or other resources to spell these words correctly.

- Teach students a variety of spelling strategies that emphasize both phonetic patterns and visual memorization. Many of these strategies can be found in the rest of this chapter.

- Avoid overdoing rules and do not hide exceptions to the rules. For example, the "*i* before *e* except after *c*" rule works in words such as *die, receive,* and *field* but does not work for *weird* or *weigh.*

- Help students to proofread their own writing and get a sense of what does not look quite right.

(Adapted from Routman, 2000; Pinnell & Fountas, 1998; Bear et al., 2000.)

☐ CLASSROOM STRATEGIES FOR SPELLING AND WRITING

SHARED (OR INTERACTIVE) WRITING

Shared writing, also called **interactive writing,** implies that students are actively involved in producing a piece of writing. This is often done on a chalkboard or chart paper with the teacher beginning the writing, and then inviting students to help by "sharing the pen." Students and teacher can work together to brainstorm ideas for writing, perhaps a letter to a local weatherman asking for information about tornado safety, or a list of rules to follow when caring for the new classroom pet. When possible, authentic purposes for writing are the best. The teacher should stop and ask for help in writing the text. The youngest students could be asked to come up and write the first letter of a word; older students could be asked to supply vowels, rime patterns, or entire words. The teacher must use professional judgment in deciding which words to use: Primary students may only help write phonetically regular high frequency words; older students might purposefully be given multisyllable irregular words for focused instruction.

WRITING JOURNALS

Writing journals have become a popular way to practice writing and spelling in today's classrooms. Journals are usually just spiral notebooks that students write in daily. Some teachers give students **prompts** consisting of questions or topics for student writing. Other teachers allow students the freedom to choose their own topics. This type of writing is usually considered personal and is not graded. Some teachers may consider it private and do not read student journals. If teachers read the journals, however, they can gain tremendous insights about their students' developmental spelling levels and get to know them better as individuals. Instead of grading journals, a teacher can respond to each student's writing with a comment about the content of the writing, such as, "I'm very sorry that your cat died," or about the mechanics of the writing, such as, "You have really learned to spell a lot of new words!" Either way, the teacher and students are communicating in a meaningful way while students become more fluent writers and readers.

WRITING WORKSHOP

A **writing workshop** is a classroom organization plan designed to emphasize the process of writing in a more authentic way. Individual student writing is done in five general, but not strictly sequential, steps.

- ■ *Prewriting* or *rehearsing* is the first stage in the writing process, and involves students brainstorming ideas and jotting down ideas that they may want to develop into a text.

- ■ *Drafting* is the second stage of the writing process and includes preliminary rough drafts of a text. It has become popular to refer to these drafts as "sloppy copies." This term is subject to the same misinterpretation as invented spelling—that it is okay to write in a sloppy, unintelligible manner—but the real purpose of drafting is to get down ideas that can later be refined. It would be helpful to show students your first drafts of papers you have written to show that they are not perfect, but still readable.

- ■ *Revising* involves improving the content of the piece of writing. In this writing stage, ask students to read their stories aloud to peer partners and ask them to comment on the story's meaning.

- ■ *Editing* is the fourth stage of the writing process, when spelling, punctuation, and other mechanical aspects of writing are found and corrected. Students should be taught to edit their own pieces first before showing them to a peer or the teacher. They can simply circle words they think might be spelled wrong; then use such resources in the room as a word wall, other texts, a spelling dictionary, or a regular dictionary to check spelling and then self-correct. Teaching students to use these resources is a responsibility of teachers.

- ■ *Publishing* is the final stage of writing, when the writing is put in a final form ranging from papers stapled together and illustrated with crayons to elaborate desktop publishing creations that are posted on a class website and shared around the world. This is the chance to celebrate each student's accomplishments as an author.

MINI LESSONS

An invaluable part of the writing workshop is the **mini lesson,** a short, focused lesson that teaches a particular skill or strategy to students. Mini lessons provide practical applications for students. Examples of spelling mini lessons are shown in Figure 6.7. Teachers might build a mini lesson around words that they notice students often misspell in their own writing, such as Paul and Kwan's problem with the word *separate,* or they could use a list of frequently misspelled words, as shown in Figure 6.8, to increase automaticity in spelling.

BUDDY STUDY SPELLING

Over the years, many teachers have been dissatisfied with the traditional routine of teaching spelling by introducing one core list on Monday and testing students on Friday. To vary this routine, some teachers have experimented with having students choose their own words. Use of this method can be motivating to students, but teachers then assume that students have the maturity to pick out words that are the most useful to learn to spell.

Another spelling concern that teachers have shared is that students may do very well on weekly spelling tests, but then misspell the same words in their own writing. In a study by Beckham-Hungler and Williams (2003), teachers

■ **FIGURE 6.7**   **Spelling Mini Lessons**

Objective: To help students develop a sense of knowing when a word is misspelled

1. Begin the lesson by showing a collection of purposely misspelled words in ads, such as *donuts, luv, thru, u, lite.* Challenge students to find the words and correct them with you.
2. Play "What Looks Right?" (Cunningham, 2000) as follows:
    a. Write two words with the same vowel sound and different spelling patterns on the board as models.

    date   wait

    b. Ask students for a rhyming word and write it with both spelling patterns.

    hate   hait

    c. Ask students to study each word and decide which one is spelled wrong. Then cross out the incorrect spelling. Repeat with other words and patterns.

    Note: There may be words that produce words with both spelling patterns, for example, *maid* and *made.*
3. Have students review their own writing and circle spellings they think may be incorrect. Check with resources and keep a chart of how many words turned out to be correct and incorrect.

■ FIGURE 6.8   Frequently Misspelled Words

acknowledgment	eligible	height	remember
acquaintance	embarrassed	horizontal	repetition
adolescent	especially	humorous	responsibility
although	exaggerate	immediately	restaurant
anticipate	except	influential	reversible
assassination	exercise	invariably	rhythm
awkward	existence	irresistible	secretary
beginning	expense	January	seize
believe	facsimile	jewelry	significance
beneficial	familiar	knowledgeable	sincerely
breathe	fascinate	leisurely	souvenir
choose	favorite	license	success
conscience	February	mortgage	thorough
convenient	finally	negotiate	tomorrow
definitely	forty	occurrence	travelled
disappear	government	particularly	Tuesday
disease	governor	pronunciation	unanimous
doesn't	guarantee	psychiatry	visibility
efficient	happened	recommend	Wednesday

attempted to improve this situation by choosing spelling words from students' writing and using them for spelling instruction. The researchers found that the students did not always reuse the "words learned" from their spelling lists in their writing, but when they did, they were often spelled correctly. Another encouraging finding was that students were often able to use the compare/contrast method to spell new words.

Pinnell and Fountas (1998) developed an innovative system for spelling, called **buddy study.** This five-step system takes advantage of the motivating effects of working with a peer and allows for a more individualized approach to spelling.

1. **Choose, Write, and Build. Mix, Fix, Mix.** In the first step, students choose words from a teacher-designated list of core words. These words are written on a spelling card, then "built" with magnetic letters. The partner mixes up the letters and then lets the other partner build them again.

2. **Look, Say, Cover, Write, Check.** The teacher prepares laminated file folders that have the top cover divided and cut into three equal sections. Each

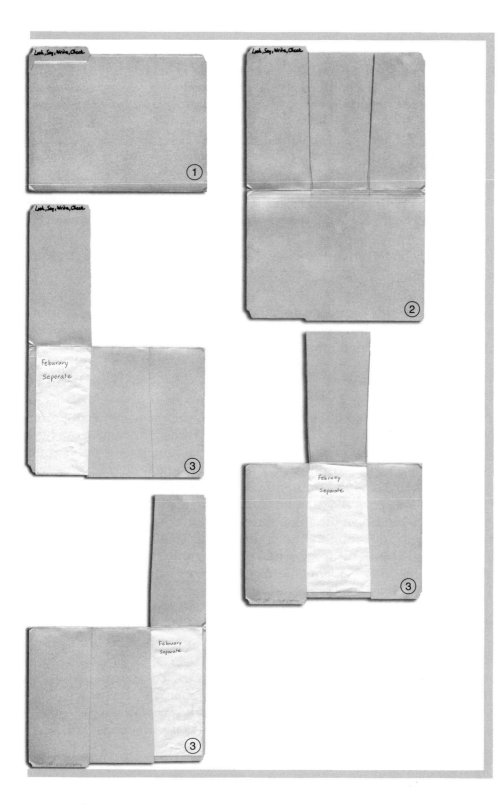

Buddy Study Look, Say, Cover, Write, Check Folder.

partner team gets a folder and puts a blank sheet of paper inside it. Partners take turns dictating their word lists to each other and studying the words, then fold up a flap and try to write the words on the paper under it.

3. **Buddy Check.** After dictating the spelling words in a context sentence, students take a highlighter pen and are taught how to mark errors and focus on troublesome parts of the word such as double letters.

4. **Make Connections.** This step encourages students to use compare/contrast methods to learn their words. For example, if a student is trying to remember the tricky spelling of *neighbor*, he might write the known word *weigh* as a connection. Memory tricks can be helpful in remembering spelling. One partner might suggest that her partner remember the phrase, "How much does my neighbor weigh?" to remind him to use the same spelling pattern.

5. **Buddy Test.** Each partner dictates and grades their partner's list of spelling words. Care must be taken that the students take this responsibility seriously.

Buddy study allows students to individualize their own learning by focusing on the words at their own spelling developmental levels. It also provides the additional benefit of motivating students by working with peers.

HIGH FREQUENCY WORD WALLS

In Chapter 4, you read about word walls being used to emphasize rime chunks. A study by Rycik (2002) found that word walls were most often used to teach recognition and spelling of high frequency words. It is not enough, however, just to display words on a word wall. They must be actively introduced and constantly used by the students. Wagstaff (1997/1998) suggests chanting or even singing the letters in a word when it is introduced and then playing a variety of word recognition games with the words each day. In one such game called "Be a Mind Reader" (Cunningham, 2000), the teacher or student secretly chooses a word on the word wall. The other students number a piece of paper from one to five. The leader gives a clue for the word, for example, "My word has one syllable," and the students must write their guesses until they come up with the secret word. Games such as this provide the kind of repeated practice needed to learn high frequency words, but without the dull routine of rote memorization.

There are several other ways word walls can be used. Routman (2000) uses personal word walls pasted to the back of student journals to help them access words that they have had difficulty spelling. Word walls can also be used for vocabulary words in content area subjects such as science, social studies, or math. Special word walls can also be constructed for easily confused words such as the homophones *their, there,* and *they're* that mystified Paul and Kwan. Mr. Allen could have students write a context sentence for each word, and perhaps even take a photograph of students demonstrating the word's meaning, such as "their car." These examples could be posted on the word wall and act as a visual reminder of each word's meaning and spelling. The rule for any kind of word wall words is the same: Once a word is posted, the students are expected to read and spell it correctly all the time.

A GLIMPSE INTO MRS. SCHLOTTERER'S FIRST-GRADE CLASSROOM

Mrs. Denee Schlotterer is conducting a whole-class mini lesson as part of her writing workshop. She has written the *-an* and *-and* rime chunks on the board and slowly says the word *can*. She asks the students, "Which family does *can* belong in?" Without hesitation, students agree to write *can* under the *-an* chunk, but then debate the next word, *hand*. Several students notice that the *-an* chunk is contained in the word *and*, but eventually they decide to put it under *-and*. Mrs. Schlotterer gives extra attention to Leia, a recent immigrant from Thailand. She knows from past experience that students whose native language is Asian often have trouble hearing the ending sounds in English words. Mrs. Schlotterer takes advantage of Leia's background knowledge by asking her the spelling of her sister Anna's name, and relating the sounds to these rime chunks. After working with several patterns, Mrs. Schlotterer ends the lesson by saying, "If you can spell these words, just think how many new words you can spell!"

The class then begins their writing. Mrs. Schlotterer puts on some soft classical music. The students get their writing folders and find comfortable places to work in the classroom or out in the hallway. Leia joins Mrs. Schlotterer on the carpet for an individual conference. She is writing a book of riddles and knock-knock jokes and is struggling with the spelling of *it's*. Mrs. Schlotterer grabs a box of magnetic letters and puts the three letters on a metal cookie sheet. She asks Leia to say each sound slowly and move the letters making that sound into the correct order. Leia is able to do this, but when she is asked to spell the word *sit* she struggles again. This time, Mrs. Schlotterer uses an ingenious device, a "phonics phone" made from two elbow joint pipes. One pipe is twisted toward Leia's ear, and the other to Mrs. Schlotterer's mouth. When she speaks the word *sit* into the phone, Leia can hear it loud and clear. She writes the word with the magnetic letters. Mrs. Schlotterer does a quick mini lesson on contractions to show Leia how to write *it's* in her book. At that, Leia leaves to continue writing on her own, and Mrs. Schlotterer begins working with the next student.

☐ TEACHER-MADE SPELLING GAMES

WHERE'S MY STUFF?

This is an appealing game for middle grade students who have trouble remembering the vowels in words.

Preparation

■ Make a game board for each player from a file folder divided into four sections labeled *clothes, food, electronics,* and *transportation.*

■ From magazines, cut out pictures for each of these categories and paste onto large index cards. Under the pictures write the name, leaving blanks for the vowels.

■ Write the vowel letters on a large wooden cube. Write "free space" on the last side.

■ Write vowel letters on individual pieces of heavy cardboard or paste over plastic pieces from an old game. Make sure to have at least 10 of each.

■ Prepare an answer key and put in an envelope.

How to Play the Game

1. Each player takes a game board and chooses a card for each section from a face-down pile. Turn the cards face up. This is now "your stuff."

Where's My Stuff? Gameboard.

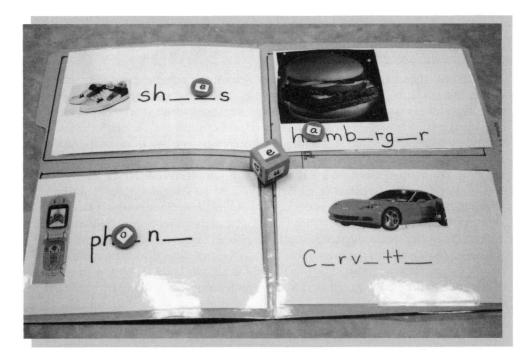

2. To keep his or her stuff, each player must, in turn, roll the die to get a letter card and put it in a correct missing vowel space.

3. If a player puts a letter in a space that another player thinks is incorrect, that player can challenge the first player. Another player should check the answer key, and the player who is wrong loses all the letters on a card.

4. The player who correctly spells all four cards is the winner.

I WON ONE

Homophones, words that sound alike but are spelled differently, are easily confused by students. The game "I Won One" helps students review the differences in meaning and spelling of homophone words. Grades 2 and up can play the game depending on word difficulty.

Preparation

- Prepare cards with different homophones used in a context sentence, for example:

  I *knew* all the answers on the test.

  They got a *new* car.

- Have a deck of player cards available. Players need paper and a pencil. Place the context sentence cards face down.

How to Play the Game

1. The teacher or a game leader chooses a card and reads it aloud to the first player without showing the card.

2. The player writes the spelling of the homophone word.

3. If correct, the student can choose a playing card randomly from the deck.

4. After a set number of rounds, players add up the point value of their playing cards (face cards = 10 points). The player with the most points is the winner.

SPELLING SURVIVOR

This is a terrific game to practice spelling high frequency words and can be adapted for any grade level.

Preparation

- Prepare, or buy, a deck of high frequency words (or other words to practice). Include cards that read "exemption from 2 misses," "good for a challenge word," and "choose someone for a challenge."

- Prepare another deck of more difficult challenge words in a different color.

- Place both decks face down in the center. Have a number of tokens, such as plastic beads, to use as points, and cards with *X*s to represent misspellings.

Spelling Survivor.

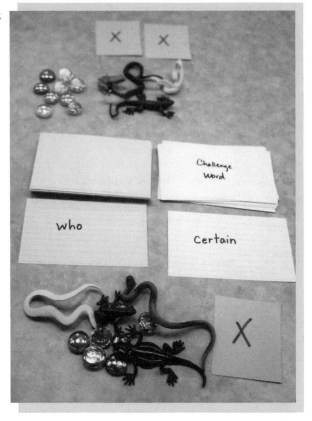

How To Play the Game

1. The first player picks a word from the regular deck. He then chooses another player to spell the word. If that player can spell it, she earns a token. If she spells it wrong, she gets a card with an *X*. If a player gets three *X*s, he is "voted out of the game."

2. If a player picks an exemption card, he can save it and use it to cancel out two misspelled words if he can successfully spell a challenge word. If a player chooses a challenge card, she can pick a challenge word and earn three tokens. If a player picks a "choose someone to do a challenge" card, he chooses another player to spell a challenge word. If that player misses, the challenger wins the three tokens.

3. Depending on time, the winner could be either the last one left in the game or the one who earned the most tokens.

INTERVENTIONS WHEN STUDENTS STRUGGLE

Spelling can be especially difficult for students with special needs. The classroom strategies for spelling and writing as outlined in this chapter can be used effectively with students who have special needs, but often more time, practice, and support is required. Read how Marcia Stoffer intervenes with a new student in her classroom.

A GLIMPSE INTO AN INTERVENTION CLASSROOM

In Marcia Stoffer's small class of intermediate students with multiple handicaps, a new student has recently joined the class. He does not know any vowel sounds and he struggles to decode words. Marcia brings out a chart of rime chunks that her students have been practicing. Each student reads a row of the chunks quite well, but when it is the new student's turn, he cannot put the sounds together. Marcia asks the other students to make the sounds of *a* and *d* so that he can successfully say the chunk *-ad*. They patiently and proudly help their fellow student to read the rest of the row.

Next, Marcia asks the students to list the numbers 1 through 5 on a piece of paper. She pronounces words using the chunks from the chart and asks the students to spell them on their papers. When the students finish, Marcia collects the papers and, without identifying the students, uses the mistakes from their papers to demonstrate corrections. For example, when a student writes *flan* for *flame*, Marcia asks, "How could you fix this?"

□ ASSESSING SPELLING

Spelling can be assessed informally by looking carefully at student writing from journals and drafts from writing workshops. Teachers can identify patterns of errors, such as problems with spelling *r*-controlled vowels or only using the CVCe pattern for long vowel words. The teacher can use this information to personalize instruction during conferences with the student.

At times, a teacher may want a more formalized spelling assessment. Bear, Invernizzi, Templeton, and Johnston (2004) have developed spelling assessments on the primary, elementary, and intermediate levels. These assessments can be used to identify the developmental level of the student, as well as the features mastered by the student and those not yet mastered, such as the complex consonant *tch*.

It is essential that students develop a sense of

Chart in Mrs. Stoffer's Intervention Classroom.

the orthographic patterns of the English language. Unfortunately, spelling is a particular challenge in English because many words, including high frequency words, have phonetically irregular spellings. Students progress through four developmental stages (prephonemic, phonemic, transitional, and conventional) as they move toward proficiency in spelling and writing. Students should be encouraged to take risks by using temporary spelling, but teachers need to directly teach students strategies that will help them become better writers. Spelling can be taught through writing formats such as shared/interactive writing, writing journals, writing workshop, or through more direct instruction using mini lessons, word walls, buddy study, games, software, or websites. In the next chapter, we look at the other features of word study, including prefixes, suffixes, and other endings.

BEFORE YOU MOVE ON

Check Your Understanding

Fill in the missing parts of this letter to parents about your writing and spelling program.

Dear Parents,

My goal this year is to help your child have the ability to recognize the familiar spelling patterns of the English language, which is called _____ _____. I will be assessing your child to determine his or her stage of developmental spelling. These stages are _____, _____, and _____. I recognize how important it is to teach writing and spelling in meaningful instructional formats, so we will be doing _____, _____, and _____ daily in our classroom. I will encourage students in the earlier stages of spelling to use _____ _____; however, my goal is to work toward immediate recognition and correct spelling of _____ _____ _____.

Sincerely,

Your Teacher

WHAT'S IN THIS CHAPTER FOR ME?

Early Childhood Teachers

Look again at the writing samples throughout the chapter. You will have students who will show amazing progress through the school year. Consider using writing portfolios to document this progress and share with your students and their parents. The shared/interactive writing model is perfect for young children who have not yet developed independent writing skills. You may not think your students will be able to keep writing journals, but even beginning kindergarteners can start with picture writing, and then proceed to using beginning consonants to represent words. Word walls have become common fixtures in today's classrooms. Take another look at the games. Which ones might be appropriate in a primary classroom? Additional spelling and writing software programs and websites are found in the appendix.

Middle Grades Teachers

Think about your own skills as a reader as opposed to a speller. If you are like most people, you can read many more words than you can spell. This explains why a middle grade student may read on grade level, but create writing full of misspellings. Look again at the description of the "transitional" and "conventional" speller. Notice that a conventional speller is not a "perfect" speller. Your students may argue that they do not need to learn to spell because they have spell-check on their computers. Using the information from this chapter, how would you answer them? Look carefully at the writing workshop format. This is a perfect way to incorporate spelling and other basic writing skills in a more authentic and enjoyable context. Read the mini lessons featured in this chapter. Think about how you might teach other spelling strategies to your students. Look also at the specific spelling activities such as buddy study and spelling games. Additional spelling and writing software and websites for middle grade students are found in the appendix. Which do you think would be the most useful to your students?

Intervention Specialists

Spelling and writing are perhaps the most difficult subjects for students with special needs. Read carefully the intervention section and the description of Marcia Stoffer's classroom for a model for helping such students. Not only may students lack the visual memory for spelling patterns, but they also may struggle with the manual dexterity necessary for writing words. For this reason, look closely at the writing and spelling software programs and "websites for kids with special needs" found in the appendix. The voice recognition software on many of these programs may allow students to use them hands free, or may be adapted to use macro keystrokes. Look again at the spelling stages. Your students will certainly make progress through these stages, but perhaps not as quickly as others in the class, and they may never reach the conventional spelling stage. Consider adapting spelling word lists to accommodate students by cutting the number of words and focusing on high frequency and phonetically regular words. The shared/interactive writing format is a perfect model for teaching writing skills in a meaningful context. Use the students' own dictated text, emphasizing their names and experiences. Word walls are also an effective strategy for students with special needs.

TEACHING WORD STRUCTURE FOR SOUND AND MEANING

Michelle Zerrer directs her fourth-grade students' attention to a special word wall in the back of the classroom. She has replaced the words that were previously displayed with seven new words. She conducts a brief review by asking, "What's special about these words?"

One student quickly answers, "They all have a prefix or suffix."

"That's right," says Mrs. Zerrer. "Now why would I want you to know them?"

One student suggests, "To help with spelling."

"To help us spell another word," answers another.

"Yes," says Mrs. Zerrer. "Learning to spell these words will also help you to spell many other words that are like them."

Mrs. Zerrer passes out "think pad" paper and tells the students to number up to seven. She tells the students that they may look at the word wall as they write the words, but she reminds them that soon they will need to write them from memory. She gives clues for each of the words on the wall, such as, "Write the word that has *cover* as a root word," and "Write the word that has a prefix that means 'against or opposed to.'" As the students write the words, Mrs. Zerrer gives them positive feedback such as, "I like how the lightbulbs are going off over your heads."

Mrs. Zerrer then asks the students to review their words and check their spellings. One student takes a meterstick and points to each word on the word wall. In unison, the other students read and spell the words aloud and correct any spelling errors they have made. Mrs. Zerrer compliments the students on their efforts, especially praising those students who were already able to spell the words without looking at the word wall.

Before you continue reading this chapter, reflect on this observation from a real classroom by considering these questions:

- What do you think Mrs. Zerrer was trying to teach her students about identifying words?
- Students said that the word wall would help their spelling. Do you agree? How might it also help their reading?
- Based on this brief sample, do you think students in this classroom are focused more on "sound" or "sense"?

As you continue reading this chapter, consider this central question: Why are lessons about prefixes, suffixes, and word roots particularly appropriate at the fourth grade and beyond?

As readers gain experience, they are able to find meaning cues within words as well as from the context of a sentence or passage. The "chunks" that they look for in words are not only phonetic elements such as a blend or a rime, but also semantic elements such as prefixes or suffixes, which are part of the meaning of the word. Knowledge about word structure can help students to access both the pronunciation and the meaning of new words. That knowledge also helps them to write longer words without having to remember their spellings letter by letter.

This chapter will show you a variety of teaching and learning activities that range from language explorations to specific skill and strategy lessons. It should also give you a new appreciation for the versatility and adaptablity of the English language.

☐ UNDERSTANDING MORPHEMES

Morphemes are the smallest meaningful units in a word. The word *unhappiness*, for instance, can be divided into three morphemes: *un, happy,* and *ness*. Morphemes can be classified as either **free morphemes,** ones that have meaning on their own, or **bound morphemes,** ones that only have meaning when attached to a root. *Happy* is a free morpheme, commonly referred to as a root word. Notice how both the form and the meaning of *happy* are "morphed" or changed by adding the bound morphemes.

When two free morphemes are connected in a single word, the result is a **compound word.** Some compound words are made of two nouns (e.g., *wallpaper*), but they may be made from other kinds of words as well (e.g., *into, everyone, however*). Sometimes morphemes are added that change the grammatical structure of a word. These **inflectional endings** include the morphemes that create plurals, possessives, contractions, and verb endings. Sometimes a single letter is all that is required to change a word from singular to plural (*boy/boys*) or from present to past (*care/cared*).

☐ STRUCTURAL ANALYSIS

Examining words to identify their free and bound morphemes, including inflectional endings, is called **morphemic analysis.** In classrooms, the process of breaking down words to understand their meaning and learn their spelling is often called **structural analysis.** Instructional activities to teach structural analysis may focus on compound words, common root words, or **affixes,** the meaningful pieces that are "fixed" or attached to a root. Affixes may be either prefixes or suffixes depending on whether they are attached before or after the root.

Teachers may give separate lessons about roots and affixes, or they may embed that instruction as students read literature, study content-area vocabulary, or write.

COMPOUND WORDS

Usually the two words that make up a compound are meaningfully related to each other, such as *football, snowman*, or *bedroom*. Other compounds have more obscure meanings, such as *butterfly* and *grapefruit*. These words are usually easy for students to recognize, but it may be harder for them to remember whether some words are written as compounds or as two separate words, as in the case of *all right* or *no one*.

PREFIXES

The most common prefixes in the English language are *un-, re-, in-, im-,* and *dis-*. These are used in 58% of words with prefixes and are, therefore, the most important ones to be taught. How many words can you make by combining these five prefixes with the following root words?

active	play	place	complete	prove	able

Prefixes are generally easy to recognize and pronounce. Students should begin to learn their meanings as soon as possible. Can you give a brief definition for each of the prefixes you just used?

SUFFIXES

Adding a suffix usually changes the part of speech of the root. For example, *teach* (verb) becomes *teacher* (noun). Common suffixes include *-able/-ible (dependable), -er/-or (sailor), -ful (cupful), -tion/-sion (confusion), -ness (kindness), -less (penniless),* and *-ship (friendship).* The spelling of the root word is sometimes changed when adding a suffix, such as in the case of *penniless.* How might you help students generate a rule to follow when adding suffixes to roots ending in *y*?

☐ TEACHING AND LEARNING ABOUT AFFIXES

Cunningham (2000) has created a "Nifty Thrifty Fifty" list of words that contain the most common prefixes and suffixes in the English language. She has also developed a clever system for teaching students how to use knowledge about one word with an affix in order to read and spell another word with the same one. Mrs. Zerrer was using this system in the lesson at the beginning of this chapter. It includes the following steps.

1. Students are introduced to a group of words from the Nifty Fifty list, such as *expensive, composer, happiness,* and *unfinished,* which may be displayed on a word wall.

2. Each word is analyzed for its meaning, and broken down into affixes and roots.

3. Students are actively involved in reviewing the words each day by clapping and "cheering" the spelling, and writing the words from clues given by the teacher, as the students in Mrs. Zerrer's class were doing.

4. Students are asked to read and write the root words from each of the target words.

5. Students rearrange the roots and affixes of the target words in order to form new words. From the five words in this example, they might create words such as *expressed, unhappiness,* and *composed.*

6. Finally, students are asked to read and write new words that combine parts of the current words with those from the previous set.

■ FIGURE 7.1   Try Out the Nifty Thrifty Fifty

Directions: Carefully examine these words created from Cunningham's list, and complete each of the activities.

unfriendly   responsibility   powerful   impression   hopeful

1. Analyze each word's prefix(es), root, and suffix(es).
2. Use your knowledge of the meanings of these word parts to write a brief definition of each word.
3. Write a clue sentence to help you remember the meaning of each word.
4. Recombine the structural elements identified in step 1 (and a few additional pieces if necessary) to create at least five new words.

Try rearranging and combining the elements of these five words with those found in the four words that were previously used as an example: *expensive, composer, happiness,* and *unfinished.*

Figure 7.1 is an activity that will give you a chance to try out Cunningham's method with a new set of words.

GREEK AND LATIN ROOTS

Students who have knowledge of common Greek and Latin roots can often unlock the meaning of many different words, especially ones in content areas. For example, the word *astronaut* was created from the Greek root *astro,* meaning "star," and *naut* meaning "sailor" (Fox, 2003). Look at the following list of common Greek and Latin roots and their meanings. How many words can you think of that have each as a morpheme? Do the morphemes always have the same meaning? How might you help students use these morphemes?

Root	Meaning	Root	Meaning
aer(o)	air, atmosphere	neo	new
anthro	human	omni	all
aqua	water	ortho	straight
aud	to hear	phon	sound
bio	life	phot	light
cycle	circle or wheel	port	carry
dem	people	psych	mind
geo	earth	quest	seek or ask
loc	place or put	scribe	write
magn	great or large	tele	distant

"Math Attack" game created by Erin Satterlee.

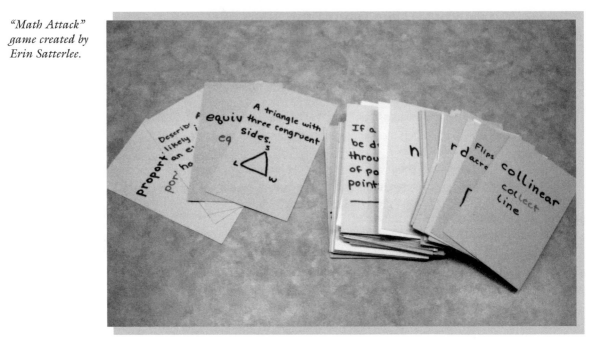

Fox (2003) advises teachers to "include in your balanced reading program often-used Greek and Latin roots that will expand children's fluent reading vocabulary" (p. 169). Learning these roots has the added benefit of helping students understand content area words such as *photosynthesis* and *millimeter*. The game pictured here is designed to help middle grade students use Greek affixes such as *milli-* to decode math content words.

TEACHING BIG WORDS IN MEANINGFUL CONTEXT

Word structure can certainly be taught through activities that focus on particular elements such as roots or affixes. Nevertheless, it is important that students see how structural analysis strategies can be applied to the books they are actually reading and the texts they are trying to write. Words taken from the novels that students are reading will tend to be be more useful and more interesting to students than those found in lists or workbooks.

For example, the *Harry Potter* books (Rowling, 1997) feature such names as Draco Malfoy, which can be compared with other words such as *Dracula* and *malevolent* to give clues to the character's traits. Rowling (1997) also invents words that have Latin morphemes, such as *portkey, lumos, impedimenta,* and *veritas serum,* that can be analyzed and compared with other words. (For more information see Nilsen and Nilsen, 2002.)

The popular *A Series of Unfortunate Events* books by Lemony Snicket also provide a wealth of opportunity for students to use their knowledge about word structure. In the ninth book, *The Carnivorous Carnival* (Snicket, 2002), words such as *ambidextrous, contortionists, hinterlands, archival,* and *carnivorous* appear and can be used to demonstrate morphemic analysis. Popular magazines, song lyrics, and advertisements all contain a surprising number of challenging words that students will be motivated to learn.

Bear et al. (2000) suggest that students keep word study notebooks in which they practice sorting and comparing words that they encounter in their reading. It is also essential that teachers model the process of analyzing words and encourage students to be "word detectives." A teacher might, for example, use the sentence, "The rabbit hid in his subterranean home until darkness fell," to conduct a "think-aloud" that shows how readers deal with words that are not in their oral language vocabularies. The think-aloud might go something like this:

> I'm not sure how to pronounce this word or what it means, but I do recognize some parts of it. *Sub* is a prefix that is at the beginning of *submarine* and *subway,* and it usually means "under." I'm not sure what the root word is, but the piece in the middle, *terra,* looks like *terrain,* and that means "ground." I'm still not sure how to pronounce it, but I think it probably means "underground." That makes sense because I think rabbits might hide underground.

Similar think-aloud lessons can demonstrate how structural pieces can be used to figure out a tentative spelling for a word that students are struggling to write.

As you have seen in previous chapters, literature circles and guided reading are natural environments for students to apply a combination of structural analysis and contextual strategies.

INFLECTIONAL ENDINGS

Understanding the ways in which words are changed in order to show plurals, possessives, and contractions is an important part of decoding for beginners and for editing writing for older students. Teachers can begin to point out these features of words to very young students during shared reading activities. As students progress, these conventions may be the focus for one-to-one editing conferences while students are writing. Teachers may also decide to do separate lessons on issues such as the ones discussed next.

PLURALS Students easily understand that plurals mean "more than one," but plurals are much more difficult to write than they are to use in speech because of the many rules governing their formation. Plurals are also confused by many children with singular possessives because they sound the same and both end in *s*. Rules for plurals include:

- Add -*s* to most words (e.g., *dogs*).
- Add -*es* to words that end in *s, sh, ch, x, z,* or long *o* as in *heroes* (not *zoos*).
- If the letter before the final *y* is a consonant, change the *y* to an *i* before adding -*es* (e.g., *babies*).
- If the letter before a final *y* is a vowel, just add -*s* (e.g., *boys*).
- If a word ends in *f* or *fe*, change it to *v* and add -*es* (e.g., *lives*).
- Some words stay the same as plurals (e.g., *deer, sheep*). Some of these words may have an *s* when referring to groups (e.g., *peoples*).
- Some words change to a different word (e.g., *child–children, foot–feet*).

POSSESSIVES Possessives can be either nouns or pronouns, singular or plural.

- A **singular possessive** is formed by adding an apostrophe and an -*s* (e.g., *Karen's book, the man's car*). If a word ends in *s* and is only one syllable, follow the same rule (e.g., *Chris's*). If the word is two syllables or more, put the apostrophe after the -*s* (e.g., *Marcus'*).
- A **plural possessive** is formed by using an apostrophe after the -*s* (e.g., *the three girls' dorm*). Even though the word *children* is plural, it uses a singular possessive form (*children's library*).
- A **possessive pronoun** does not use an apostrophe (e.g., *his, her, its, their, our*).

These words can be very confusing to students. In Figure 7.2, you will see as example of a mini lesson to teach the difference between plural and possessive words.

VERB ENDINGS There are certain rules for adding inflectional endings to verbs.

- *The 1-1-1 rule*. For words with one syllable, one short vowel, and one ending consonant, double the consonant before adding an ending that begins with a vowel (e.g., *run–running, step–stepped*).
- *Verbs ending in a silent* e. Drop the *e* before adding an ending that begins with a vowel (e.g., *bake–baking, smile–smiled*).
- *Verbs ending in* y *are tricky*. Sometimes the *y* is changed to an *i* as in *tries*, but when -*ing* is added, the *y* may remain, as in *trying*. This is done here to avoid a double *i*, but not in the case of the word *skiing*.
- *Adding* -ed *to most verbs*. This will change the verb to past tense, but the pronunciation varies [e.g., *landed* (/ed/ sound), *walked* (/t/ sound)].

■ FIGURE 7.2 Plural/Possessive Mini Lesson

After students have been introduced to both plural and possessive forms, it is helpful to mix practice of both of them to ensure that they can understand the different usage. One way to do this is to guide students in proofreading and correcting pieces of writing during which time students are gradually given less help in finding the errors. For example, a first sentence might be:

Sarahs dog ran away while she was walking near the **house's** down the block.

The bold words would cue students where to find the mistakes, and the teacher would model correcting the mistakes as a whole class. Next, the students might be given a sentence like this:

Sarah found the dogs collar in the bush's and several of its hair's on the leafs.

The class would be divided into small groups and told to find four mistakes in the sentence and then correct them together.

Finally, students would be given sentences to do independently with no cues to guide them as to the number of mistakes. An additional activity would be for students to write their own sentences, purposefully making mistakes, and exchange them with another student who would find and correct the mistakes.

SPELLING WORDS WITH SUFFIXES In many cases, suffixes can be added to a word without difficulty. The *-ful* suffix is one example. Teachers must be aware, however, of a few points.

- Adding *-er* or *-est* will change an adjective into a comparative adjective (e.g., *smart–smarter, happy–happiest*).
- Some suffixes sound the same, but have different spellings (e.g., *nation–confusion, miserable–terrible, radius–wondrous*).

CONTRACTIONS Contractions can be explained to students simply as a shortcut way to make two words into one by removing some of the letters. They may, however, still confuse contractions with possessives because both use apostrophes. Common contractions are formed using *am* (*I'm*), *us* (*let's*), *are* (*you're*), *had* or *would* (*I'd, she'd*), *is* or *has* (*he's, who's*), *will* (*I'll*), *have* (*I've*), and *not* (*didn't*). When a contraction is formed with *not*, the *n* is attached to the first word. Some contractions are irregular (e.g., *will–won't*).

Try your hand at creating your own mini lesson (see Figure 7.3).

☐ INTERVENTIONS WHEN STUDENTS STRUGGLE

Several approaches to word identification have been developed to help students with special needs. Polloway, Polloway, and Serna (2001) created the

■ Figure 7.3   Make Your Own Learning Activity

Plan a learning activity for your classroom by following these steps.

1. Choose a skill from this list:
   - Adding endings to words ending in *y*
   - Distinguishing between pronoun possessives like *its* and contractions like *it's*
   - Irregular plurals
   - Distinguishing between contractions like *you're* and possessives like *your*
   - When to double ending consonants
   - When to drop a silent *e*
   - How to spell similar suffixes
   - Understanding easily confused words like *we're* and *were*
2. Choose how you will directly teach this skill. What words will you use to demonstrate it? What format will you use?
3. Plan how you will directly involve your students in practicing this skill in a way that is not simply rote memorization. How will you get feedback from all of your students?
4. Plan a way to assess whether all your students have learned this skill. How will you know they have learned what you taught them?

CRUSCH word identification strategy for students with special needs. Each letter stands for a strategy that students can do to help themselves when trying to figure out a word.

Consonant. Focus on the beginning consonant.

Rapid. Rapidly check vowel sounds, prefixes, and suffixes while reviewing the word.

Unimportant. Skip over words that do not require practice.

Syllabicate. Apply chunking strategies if the word is important.

Context. Use the context to help with meaning.

Help. Seek help from the teacher, peer, or dictionary.

□ Syllables and Accents

A **syllable** is a basic unit of pronunciation, and as such, can only contain one vowel phoneme. Therefore, the number of vowel sounds in a word is equal to the number of syllables in a word. Learning activities for syllables can range from basic to quite advanced. For example, a kindergartner can be taught to recognize and clap the number of syllables (or beats) in a word. This is a basic phonemic awareness activity. At the other end of the spectrum, an eighth grader can learn to divide a multisyllable word into syllables and identify the primary and secondary accents. The goal in both cases is to help the students become more proficient at reading and writing words, not become an expert in syllable division. Syllables are comparable to *chunks* in words, and helping students to recognize those chunks will make them better readers and writers. Rules for dividing words into syllables can be complicated and confusing. Following are the most basic and useful rules.

- If the first syllable has a short vowel sound, divide after the consonant (e.g., *sev-en*).
- If the first syllable has a long vowel sound, divide after the vowel (e.g., *de-stroy* or *a-corn*).
- If the word has two consonants in the middle of the word, divide between them (e.g., *won-der*).
- Divide prefixes and suffixes from the root word (e.g., *im-prove-ment*).

In multisyllable words, syllables receive different **accent** or **stress;** in other words, we say one syllable louder or with more emphasis. Say the word *rabbit* aloud and you will notice that you pronounce it ***rab****-bit* rather than *rab-**bit.*** Interestingly, certain words in the English language can have different meanings depending on which syllable is stressed. For example, the word *produce* can mean either "fruits and vegetables" or "to make something," depending on which syllable is accented. Figure 7.4 includes some funny examples of this phenomenon.

Pronunciation of multisyllable words is complicated by the fact that most vowel sounds in unaccented syllables are schwa sounds and are not distinctive. By analyzing which syllables are accented, students can have some assurance that accented syllables will usually have a clear vowel sound and be easier to

■ **FIGURE 7.4**   **Why the English Language Is So Hard to Learn**

Read these sentences in which a word is pronounced two different ways depending on the accent. Consider how difficult it would be for an English language learner to understand them.

1. The bandage was wound around the wound.
2. He could lead if he would get the lead out.
3. The dump was so full that it had to refuse more refuse.
4. This is a good time to present the present.
5. They were too close to the door to close it.
6. To help with the planting, the farmer taught his sow to sow.
7. After a number of injections, my jaw got number.
8. The wind was too strong to wind the sail.
9. When shot at, the dove dove into the bushes.

pronounce and spell. Students in the middle grades need to be taught how to understand the markings for primary (´) and secondary accents in the dictionary. If you feel it is necessary for students to also learn how to accent words themselves, the following are no-nonsense rules.

- The primary accent is most likely to be on the first syllable.
- Prefixes and suffixes are usually not accented.
- With words that can be pronounced two ways (see Figure 7.4), nouns are usually accented on the first syllable (*ob´ject*), verbs on the second (*ob ject´*).
- If the last syllable has a long vowel pair, it is usually accented (*ex plain´*).

□ ASSESSING AFFIXES

Using the following list of words, teachers can assess student ability to understand words with common prefixes and suffixes. Students can be asked to read the words, spell them, identify the affixes and roots, and/or explain any spelling changes to the root.

1. preview	7. unicorn	13. indirect
2. bicycle	8. expectation	14. hotter
3. ugliest	9. rewind	15. uncovered
4. octagonal	10. misspell	16. forecast
5. disobey	11. happily	17. plentiful
6. carelessness	12. wiser	18. penniless

□ BUILDING A RICH VOCABULARY KNOWLEDGE

It is pointless for students to decode a word if they have no idea about its meaning. A student's vocabulary is closely linked with background knowledge and experiences. Effective vocabulary study involves integrating new word meanings with existing knowledge in meaningful ways. Rupley, Logan, and Nichols (1998/1999) suggest selecting words for study from classroom texts, creating activities that focus on word meanings in multiple contexts, comparing features of known words to unknown ones, and using analogies, word mapping, webbing, and even kinesthetic associations such as touch and smell to visualize words.

■ **FIGURE 7.5**   Vocabulary Contest

The *Reader's Digest* National Word Power Challenge is similar to the National Spelling Bee, but tests students in grades 4 through 8 on their ability to master vocabulary words. Students compete on the local and state level before qualifying for the national championship held in Orlando, Florida. The contest awards $50,000 in college scholarships. For more information, go to *wordpowerchallenge.com.*

Students experience a sense of power and accomplishment when they can master long or difficult vocabulary words. One way to do this is to select vocabulary words from a text or content area, and then challenge students to find the meanings and use them correctly in a context sentence, either oral or written. Students could set a personal goal for learning new words, and when they have attained that goal, win a reward. Another source of difficult words is *allwords.com*, which features a "Word of the Week." A definition, discussion, etymology, and foreign translation for each word is presented in an interesting way. For example, the word *pusillanimous* is discussed in terms of the pusillanimous (or cowardly) lion from *The Wizard of Oz.*

Your students may be motivated to demonstrate their new found word skills by entering the contest as shown in Figure 7.5.

☐ INTERESTING WORDS

It is important that teachers inspire in students a love for words and impart strategies for working with them. As Rasinski and Padak (2001) put it, "Behind all this instruction and activity is the idea that students need to learn these important word patterns, but also that students develop an intense fascination with words—to become wordsmiths" (p. 72). The objective of helping students to enjoy words and become wordsmiths should not be dismissed as frivolous. The more students are engaged in using words in a fun and playful way, the more likely they are to want to read and write on their own; and conversely, when students are doing only meaningless tasks in the classroom, they are unlikely to be excited about words. In our quest to help students meet standards of proficiency, it is equally important to encourage them to become lifelong lovers of language. The following examples promote fun encounters with interesting words.

NEW WORDS AND SLANG

Students may not be aware that new words are added to our lexicons each year that reflect our culture as English-speaking people. Among the new entries to *Merriam Webster's Collegiate Dictionary* (2003) are words that have become part of our everyday life such as *Botox*, and *dot-comers*, and ones that need some explanation. *Dead presidents* is a new-age term for money; *Frankenfood* is genetically modified food; *McJob* refers to a low-paying job that requires little skill and no hope for advancement; *phat* means good or highly attractive; and *dead-cat bounce* is a brief, but insignificant bounce back from an economic loss. So if a guy spends all his dead presidents from his McJob making Frankenfood on some phat chick, you can now decide whether to give him a dead-cat bounce. Slang words such as these are included in the dictionary when they begin to turn up regularly on the internet and in text sources such as newspapers, magazines, and books.

Slang words often reflect new developments in the history or culture of the people using the language. The term *big cheese* originated from the Persian or Hindi word *chiz* which means "a thing." British people living in India in the 19th century used it in sentences like, "My horse is the real chiz." When they returned to England, *chiz* became *cheese*. In America, the term *big cheese* was first used by Ring Lardner in his novels to indicate an important person.

Slang often emerges during wartime. During the Civil War, *bread basket* meant stomach, *sawbones* was a doctor, and *skedaddle* meant to run away. Likewise, during the Vietnam War, soldiers called their meals *beans*, *green* meant safe, and a *believer* was a dead soldier.

Worldwidewords.com has an excellent section on slang origins. From here you can learn that the word *cooties* can be traced to a biting insect from Malay and that it was first used to describe body lice during World War I well before it became a playground taunt.

ETHNIC HERITAGE

Approximately 80% of our words derive from other languages (McCrum, MacNeil, & Cran, 2002). Just as America is a fascinating smorgasbord of races, religions, and cultures, the English language is a stewpot full of different word origins.

One way to get students excited about word origins is to ask them to research words that have entered the language through their own particular ethnic heritage. One place to start is the *worldwidewords.com* website which includes an index of words and their origins and support pages including a "Contact the Author" feature. Figure 7.6 is a partial list of words that have evolved from other languages.

English can even seem different to other English Speakers. Read Figure 7.7 to see how American English differs from British English.

■ FIGURE 7.6   English Words from Other Languages

SPANISH	FRENCH	DUTCH	ARABIC	HINDI	GERMAN	ITALIAN
barbecue	bayou	waffle	mattress	shampoo	hamburger	ballerina
chocolate	depot	coleslaw	Algebra	dungarees	snorkel	soprano
tomato	gopher	cookie	numeral	pajamas	waltz	casino
enchilada	cuisine	landscape	number		kindergarten	broccoli
plaza	boutique	sleigh			cookbook	pizza
stampede	chauffeur	boss			hoodlum	pasta
tornado					ecology	espresso

■ FIGURE 7.7   Whose Language Is It, Anyway?

You may think you speak English, but American English is quite different from British English. Not only are there differences in spelling (*color* and *colour*) and usage (*while* and *whilst*), but also the words may be entirely different, as noted here.

American	British	American	British
apartment	flat	hood of car	bonnet
argument	row	Jello	jelly
baby carriage	pram	jelly	jam
band-aid	plaster	lawyer	solicitor
bathroom	loo or WC	line	queue (Q)
can	tin	mail	post
cookie	biscuit	movie theatre	cinema
dessert	pudding	muffler	silencer
diaper	nappy	napkin	serviette
elevator	lift	nothing	nought
flashlight	torch	parking lot	car park
fries	chips	pharmacist	chemist
gas	petrol	potato chips	crisps
guy	bloke, chap	sausage	banger
hamburger meat	mince	truck	lorry
highway	motorway	vacation	holiday

WORDS OF THE YEAR

Every year since 1990 the American Dialect Society (ADS) has chosen a word of the year that best represents the culture and politics of that particular year. A listing of the words and explanations can be found on their website at *www.americandialect.org.* On January 7, 2005, members voted in the phrases *red states, blue states,* and *purple states,* referring to the colors representing majority political parties during the 2004 election. Runner-ups included *flip-flopper, wardrobe malfunction,* and *phish* (which means "to acquire passwords or other private information via digital ruse"). Past winners reflect current events in the news such as *weapons of mass destruction* in 2002, *9-11* in 2001, *chad* in 2000, and *Y2K* in 1999. Students could search newspapers and newsmagazines for a particular year to discover the context for which these words were used and why they were significant. Students might also hold their own election for words that have been important in a year and compare it to the ADS list.

☐ SPECIALIZED WORDS

IDIOMS

English speakers have created hundreds of idioms that make our language unique and often puzzling to those trying to learn it. Americans understand when we tell each other to "knock it off," but imagine how this phrase could easily be misinterpreted by an English language learner. *Wordorigins.org* traces the meaning of 400 words and phrases. *Wordwizard.com* has a discussion group on the origin of various words and phrases where participants can join in an argument about the origin of the phrase *pirates' booty* or learn about what a *frog march* is. (It's a term for holding a drunken prisoner face down with a person holding each limb.) Finally, speaking of frogs, Leedy and Street (2003) have written a wonderful picture book called *There's a Frog in My Throat! 440 Animal Sayings a Little Bird Told Me.* In it, idioms (and similes, metaphors, and proverbs) are organized according to animals—from dogs ("it's a dog's life," "don't bite the hand that feeds you," and "his tail between his legs") to ducks ("sitting duck," "duck soup," and "silly goose").

Two books by Fred Gwynne, *The King Who Rained* (1970) and *A Chocolate Moose for Dinner* (1976), use idioms such as "frog in her throat" to illustrate their literal meaning. Other words used in the books are homophones such as *horse* and *hoarse, bear* and *bare, boars* and *bores, pray* and *prey,* and *rained* and *reigned.* A teacher can supply explanations of the book's lesser-known idioms and phrases such as "arms race," "on the lam," "row in shells," and "gamble on the lawn," and encourage students to find the spelling of homophones such as *mousse* and *guerilla.*

OXYMORONS

Oxymorons are two words that appear to contradict each other, such as *bittersweet* and *cruel kindness*, yet are meaningful in context. Sometimes these words are used as a punch line of a joke, such as *military intelligence*. A list of these words can be found at *fun-with-words.com*. Students can create their own oxymoron books using the Gwynne and Leedy books as models. For example, they might illustrate *open secret* by showing a person whispering to another into a microphone on the Jerry Springer show.

PALINDROMES AND PORTMANTEAUS

Palindromes are words or phrases that are spelled the same backwards and forwards. Although it is quite challenging to write their own, younger students can identify single-word palindromes such as *mom, dad, madam,* and *Hannah*. Older students may be able to read and create their own palindromes. Students can write palindrome sentences if they have models. The most clever are by John Agee. The titles of his books are all memorable palindromes: *Go Hang a Salami. I'm a Lasagna Hog!* (1994), *So Many Dynamos* (1994), and *Sit on a Potato Pan, Otis!* (1999). The books are illustrated with delightful drawings. Other palindrome words can be found on *fun-with-words.com*.

Portmanteaus are words that are shortened from two words. These include such words as *brunch, clash, smog,* and *squiggle*. Students may enjoy coining their own words using parts of two words such as *frisfoot* (football played with a Frisbee).

□ □ □ □ □

BEFORE YOU MOVE ON

Check Your Understanding

Sort each of the following terms into one of three categories: Word Analysis, Word Play, or The English Language.

palindromes	free morphemes	affixes
bound morphemes	portmanteaus	prefixes
verb endings	plurals and possessives	slang
suffixes	Greek and Latin roots	idioms
ethnic heritages	compound words	oxymorons
syllables	accents	

WHAT'S IN THIS CHAPTER FOR ME?

Early Childhood Teachers

Reread this chapter so that you are knowledgeable and confident in your ability to teach the word structures presented here to your students. By the end of primary grades, your students will be expected to do simple morphemic analysis such as identifying the prefix, suffix, and root; to read and write most plurals, possessives, and contractions; and to know and use simple rules for verb endings such as doubling the consonant and changing *y* to *i*.

Students as young as kindergarten should be able to hear the number of syllables in a word, and older primary students can use their knowledge of syllables to chunk a word when spelling. The challenge of teaching primary grades is to break down a concept into small, manageable steps that young children can follow. Read Figure 7.2 again for a model of how this is done. Then look at Figure 7.3 and choose a skill that would be appropriate for the grade you intend to teach. How would you break this down into manageable steps?

Middle Grade Teachers

Reread this chapter so that you are knowledgeable and confident in your ability to teach the word structures presented here to your students. You will be expected to teach your students to become proficient in morphemic analysis. However, they will no doubt still be confused by suffixes that sound the same but are spelled differently such as in *confusion* and *navigation*, and by words with inflectional endings that are similar to other words such as *we're/were*, *its/it's*, *your/you're*, or *whose/who's*.

Review the section on "Inflectional Endings." Choose a skill that would be appropriate to the grade level you intend to teach. How could you help students learn these different kinds of words? Look again at Figure 7.1. This list of the Nifty Thrifty Fifty could be very valuable to your teaching. Try answering the questions at the bottom. The teacher in the opening scenario was teaching these words. Be sure to also check out the student-made middle grade games and try your hand at creating a learning activity in Figure 7.3.

The sections, "Teaching Big Words in Meaningful Context" and "Interesting Words," were especially written with middle grades in mind. Be sure to check out the websites and fun ideas in Figures 7.5, 7.6, and 7.7 to help you motivate your students to enjoy words and learn more about them.

Intervention Specialists

Reread this chapter so that you are knowledgeable and confident in your ability to teach the word structures presented here to your students. Learning the skills described in this chapter requires practice and multiple exposures. This is especially true for your students who often have difficulty retaining information. Your challenge is to make this practice interesting and memorable. Carefully read the intervention section on the CRUSCH strategy and check out the special needs websites in the Appendix.

Review the sections on compounds, plurals, possessives, and contractions. How might you teach these words in a way that your students would remember them? Consider acting out adding an *s* when *cat* becomes *cats*, or having *it* and *is* collide to make *it's*. The use of colors to emphasize the differences in words can also be effective. Check out the picture books described in the chapter by Leedy and Gwynne. Find pictures to show your students and let them explain why they are funny, such as "a frog in my throat."

ACCOMMODATING AND SUPPORTING STUDENTS WITH LANGUAGE DIFFERENCES

M onica Carrera-Wilburn is a primary grade teacher in Arizona with a large number of students who are still learning the English language. She guides them to brainstorm ideas for writing bilingual books called "Welcome to Room 25" by asking them, "What do we want people to know about us?" Each student works with a partner to answer that question, one writing in English and the other in Spanish.

Because Ms. Carrera-Wilburn wants her students to focus on writing the text more than drawing the pictures, the students cut out pictures from magazines to illustrate their books. She tells them to "make sure your pictures match your words."

When the students are finished, their bilingual books become their books for independent and buddy reading as well as an integral part of the classroom's library. Ms. Carrera-Wilburn's class has shown that *English language learners* can participate in all aspects of literacy.

As she is fond of telling them, "If I can hear it, and speak it, and understand it, then I can read it."

Before you continue reading, take a moment to reflect on the following questions:

■ What opportunities does this activity provide for students to hear and speak English informally?

■ How does this activity help students to learn about letters and sounds and the structure of words?

■ How is this activity similar to those that would be done with more "typical" students? How is it different?

☐ ☐ ☐ ☐ ☐

As you continue reading this chapter, think about the instructional practices that best accommodate student differences in knowledge of English as well as the differences in pronunciation, vocabulary, and syntax shown by speakers of various English dialects.

The main concern of this book is developing the knowledge and strategies that students need in order to recognize words they already know and to identify words that are unfamiliar or even totally new. Students take many years to accomplish these tasks, even when the language they are trying to read and write is the same as their families use at home. Learning phonics and word identification is even more challenging for students who must master new sounds, syntax, and vocabulary at the same time. In this chapter, we examine the challenges faced by students who are learning English and identify principles and practices that help these students to learn and use new language forms. We also examine issues related to the diverse dialects and forms of English and suggest guidelines for giving all students equal opportunities to learn.

☐ UNDERSTANDING THE NEEDS OF ENGLISH LANGUAGE LEARNERS

The term *English language learner (ELL)* refers to "children born in the United States or in other countries who are from homes where the primary language spoken is not English (Grant & Wong, 2003). This term has replaced earlier labels such as English as a second language (ESL) or limited English proficient (LEP), because it reflects more clearly that these individuals have a great deal of knowledge about their first language and some knowledge of English, although they are still learning.

Between 1986 and 1998, the number of students in the United States who were still learning English rose from 1.6 million to 9.9 million [International Reading Association (IRA), 2001]. By the year 2050, the percentage of school-age children who speak a language other than English will reach 40% (Lindholm-Leary, 2000). Clearly, reading teachers need to know techniques for assessment and instruction that meet the special needs of English language learners. The first step is a thorough understanding of the obstacles that their ELL students have already overcome and the challenges they still face.

Instruction and assessment of phonics and word identification cannot be separated from concern with the overall language development of ELL students. As Ms. Carrera-Wilburn points out to her class, reading English is closely tied to speaking and understanding English. In this section, we describe factors that are crucial to understanding the range of abilities and challenges represented among these students. We also suggest ways in which teachers can gather information about these factors to plan appropriate instruction.

LITERACY IN THE PRIMARY LANGUAGE

English language learners who have previously begun to read in their **primary language** have a decided advantage over those who have not, although they still face many challenges. The youngest students are least likely to be readers, simply because they have had fewer years in which to learn. Older readers, however, have sometimes missed the opportunity to learn. Economic hardships or political unrest may have disrupted the schooling of recent immigrants, or they may come from cultures that are not highly literate.

Some students who were born in America, including children of migrant workers, may have received only sporadic instruction. To accurately assess the progress of ELL students, teachers need to investigate their educational backgrounds as much as possible, although this can be difficult.

DEVELOPING CONVERSATIONAL ENGLISH PROFICIENCY

Some English language learners have already developed the ability to understand everyday English and to make themselves understood in conversation. For others, this is a challenging task. Developing conversational ability in English requires opportunities to interact with others, but English language learners may shy away from interactions with others because they are afraid of making mistakes in pronunciation or of misunderstanding what others are saying.

Even in their primary language, children can generally understand more than they can say, but when English language learners avoid speaking, others may underestimate their knowledge or ability to learn. Teachers must observe English language learners carefully to judge whether they are understanding, and they need to encourage students to be open about showing when they do not understand.

Developing Academic English Proficiency

Researchers have found that most ELL students can learn conversational English in about 2 years; however, it may take 5 to 7 years to acquire the academic proficiency in English needed to understand content-area information (Drucker, 2003). Cummins (1994) identified two factors that make academic language hard to learn—context and cognitive complexity. Learning words is easiest when they are concrete and tied to specific situations and experiences. Words about food, for instance, are easier to learn than words about economics, and learning words associated with cooking can most easily be done while preparing a meal.

Academic language tasks often present a high degree of complexity with little context. Especially in content classes, English language learners are often required to learn about objects and events that are not present in the room or part of their personal or cultural experience. The meaning is **decontextualized.** They need to develop the general reading and writing ability that is necessary to do school assignments. In addition, they must acquire the specific vocabulary that is used in different content areas and become familiar with the organization and style of various textbooks.

Social and Cultural Transitions

Language is closely bound to culture, and English language learners are often caught on a borderline between two cultures as well as two languages. They may often find that the customs and traditions that go with their new language are incomprehensible. Imagine, for instance, trying to understand Valentine's Day if it was a totally new idea presented in an unfamiliar language.

ELL students may be responsible for helping adults at home to negotiate a new culture at the same time they are learning to do so themselves. Teachers must be sensitive to differences in culture as well as language, especially the issue of **cultural abandonment,** the conflict that English language learners may feel between taking on a new culture and respecting their native culture (Grant & Wong, 2003).

☐ Phonetic and Graphic Differences Between Languages

Learning English is easier for some students than it is for others, because the general form of their language is similar to that of English. ELL students will have difficulty, for instance, with English phonemes that do not exist in their native language. They will tend to substitute other familiar sounds. One example is the /r/ phoneme, which does not exist in Japanese. A Japanese student is likely to substitute an /l/ sound as in pronouncing *glass* instead of *grass*. Students from India have a similar problem distinguishing /v/ from /w/.

English language learners who have learned to read in their own languages may still find challenges in decoding written English. Grant and Wong (2003) point out that the kinds of processing done in reading other languages might not be the same as those required for English. They note, for example, that the alphabetic system (each sound represented by a letter) does not apply to Chinese and that classical Chinese does not use punctuation to mark the end of a sentence.

Students whose first languages are based on Latin or German may have an easier time learning English. Spanish speakers, for instance, who usually make up a large portion of the English language learners in American schools, will find many **cognates** (words that are written or pronounced almost the same) in English. Nevertheless, important differences exist in the use of sounds and symbols, and those differences complicate the process of word identification. Figure 8.1 compares Spanish and English phonemes.

Even if you do not speak Spanish, it is useful to know the phonemes that language has in common with English so that you can start word identification instruction with words that have those common phonemes. Keep in mind that students from different Spanish-speaking countries such as Mexico, Puerto Rico, or from South American countries will speak different versions of Spanish.

Nilsen and Nilsen (2004) suggest a series of vocabulary lessons organized around English words that share a relationship with Spanish. They describe, for instance, how the root *man* in English words such as *manuscript* and *manufacture* is related to the Spanish *mano*, which means "hand." Spanish speakers can see their own language being used and can contribute Spanish words that use the same root.

☐ ASSESSING ENGLISH LANGUAGE LEARNERS

Garcia (1994) points out that neither standardized tests of language proficiency nor state and local proficiency tests may give teachers the information they need to plan effective instruction for English language learners. She suggests instead a mix of authentic assessment procedures that includes classroom observations using anecdotal records or charts to track oral and written language use as well as tools such as oral miscue analysis, story retellings, and tape-recorded oral reading to determine fluency and expressiveness in English or even in the student's first language.

Helman (2005) used the results from 18,000 students taking the Phonological Awareness Literacy Screening (PALS) to provide information on the best ways to improve the teaching of English language learners. Helman made the following conclusions.

■ FIGURE 8.1   Comparing Spanish Phonemes to English

Common Consonant Sounds

/b/	/f/	/g/	/k/	/l/
/m/	/n/	/p/	/s/	/t/
/w/	/y/	/ch/	/pl/	/pr/*
/fr/*	/br/*	/tr/*	/dr/*	/gr/*
/cr/*	/fl/	/cl/	/bl/	/gl/

* /r/ sound will be trilled; h is silent.

English Consonant Phonemes Not Found in Spanish

English Phoneme	Likely Substitute for Spanish Speakers
/d/	/th/ (voiced)
/j/	/ch/
/r/	trilled sound or /w/, /u/
/v/, /z/, /th/	/b/
/sh/	/ch/
blends beginning with *s*	adding an *e* before the *s*

Spanish vowels are more consistent than English ones because they are more likely to have a one-to-one correspondence between letter and sound. Spanish and English have several vowel phonemes in common, but they may be spelled differently.

Vowel	Spelling in English	Spelling in Spanish
a (L)	make	hecho
e (L)	beat	ido
i (L)	bike	aire
o (L)	note	ocho
o (S)	not	ajo
u (L)	tune	usted

Spanish does not have four of the English short vowel sounds: *a, e, i,* or *u.* Neither does it have *r*-controlled vowels, schwas, or the vowel sounds in *wood* (oo) or *caught* (aw). Not surprisingly, English words with these vowels could prove difficult for Spanish speakers.

Source: Adapted from Helman (2005).

■ FIGURE 8.2   Questions to Consider for Teachers of English Language
Learners

- How well does the student understand basic oral language, such as directions, in concrete (high context) situations?
- How well can the student speak and be understood in concrete (high context) situations?
- Can the student easily pronounce common English words?
- Can the student read and write in his or her first language?
- Can the student recognize and/or write basic function or "sight words" in English?
- Can the student recognize and/or write high frequency, phonetically regular words?
- How similar is the student's primary language to English? (Is it alphabetic? Structured by word order? Are there many cognates?)
- Is English understood, spoken, read, and/or written by the student's caregivers at home?
- What social and cultural barriers may the student be facing in addition to learning English?

■ Schools must use assessments to identify students in need of extra help.

■ Instruction must be provided on the students' developmental levels.

■ Instruction should focus on those elements that are the most difficult for students (i.e., differences in graphemes and phonemes in different languages).

■ Students must be identified early and given "enriched learning opportunities."

Figure 8.2 lists questions that teachers of English language learners should attempt to answer through informal assessment.

☐ ENVIRONMENTS FOR SUPPORTING ENGLISH LANGUAGE LEARNING

Effective classroom environments for English language learners meet the three goals set by Teachers of English to Speakers of Other Languages (TESOL): developing social language, developing academic language, and developing sociocultural knowledge. English language learners will be most successful in classrooms that surround them with oral and written English, encourage social interaction with other students, and respect their primary language and culture. The following are suggestions for creating these environments.

SURROUND ALL STUDENTS WITH ORAL AND WRITTEN LANGUAGE

Although English language learners certainly need specific instruction in the sounds and structures of English, they can learn much by continual exposure to language that is developmentally appropriate. The following suggestions will help to create a language-rich environment.

■ *Read to students and have them read orally.* When you read aloud to your students, you demonstrate English syntax, vocabulary, and pronunciation in a meaningful context. This is especially true if students follow along in their own books while you read. They may then use your oral reading as a model for practicing their own reading. Listening centers that feature recorded books serve the same purpose. Be careful, though, to choose recordings that match the text exactly.

Oral reading activities that involve repeated reading of the texts allow students time to master the vocabulary and syntax of the material while building sight vocabulary and noticing patterns within words. Hadaway, Vardell, and Young (2001) found that poetry and choral reading were especially useful to help ELL students develop fluency. Choral reading involves treating the oral reading of a poem or other text like a choral performance in music. This allows for a mix of reading in a group and limited "solo" reading.

■ *Make use of gestures and simple dramatic activities.* The gestures that naturally accompany oral language can contribute greatly to vocabulary development. When making oral explanations of content-material or during read-alouds, make sure to hold up objects and to use movement, hand gestures, and facial expressions when possible to emphasize meaning.

Herrell and Jordan (2004) suggest that English language learners can work with English speakers to "act out" a passage as it is read aloud for the class. This technique can reinforce understanding of content-area material such as the process of cell division, and it also reinforces word identification as English language learners match their actions to the words on the page.

■ *Use visuals to teach concepts, words, and spelling patterns.* Visual elements such as pictures, media, and real-world objects can play an important role in learning new vocabulary. Label objects around the room in English and in other languages. This allows native English speakers to learn new languages, as well as reinforcing their own. Bulletin boards can feature displays of pictures that are labeled and also described. A picture of a cat, for instance, could be accompanied by the words *pet, paws, whiskers,* and *fur.*

Word walls perform a variety of useful functions in classrooms for all ages. A word wall may contain high-frequency words for spelling, content vocabulary for the current unit, or words that show common structural elements such as the same roots or affixes. Charts of spelling patterns provide constant reminders of the forms of English words. Make use of familiar environmental text such as fast-food menus, movie posters, and TV guides to learn words. Gonzalez-Bueno (2003) suggests making environmental print alphabet posters.

ENCOURAGE SOCIAL INTERACTION

English language learners who are still developing conversational English should be encouraged in every way to interact with peers. Experts often suggest assigning an English language learner a buddy, preferably one who speaks the same language, to act as a guide and mentor. This strategy backfired, however, in one middle grade classroom (Fu, 2004) when the mentor students complained, "We are tired of always helping others; we want to learn and need time to do our own work" (p. 13).

The teacher modified his plan by assigning peers who could help orient the ELL student to classroom routines, some students to act as translators, and other students who would speak only English.

A variety of literacy activities can be used that encourage or require interaction. Some involve practicing a skill with a single "buddy" and others involve working with a small group.

Paired reading allows English language learners to both hear and pronounce English words as well as to recognize them on a page. It is a good follow-up to listening to a teacher read aloud or shared reading because students will have a good idea of the overall meaning of the text. Paired reading is a "safe" activity for English language learners as long as they have a supportive partner. If necessary, the pair can use "echo reading," a process where the more proficient reader reads a sentence and the English language learner immediately reads the same sentence.

Small group activities allow the greatest opportunity for English language learners to hear and use academic language. When groups are involved in creating a project, for instance, ELL students can be involved with drawing and constructing concrete objects as they apply content area concepts and language.

Herrel and Jordan (2004) state that **guided reading groups** are especially useful for English language learners. In guided reading, teachers form temporary groups based on students' needs and meet with those groups to listen to oral reading, ask clarifying questions, and provide strategy instruction. The small group allows teachers to do individual coaching in pronunciation, to clarify word meanings, and to correct misunderstandings. Guided reading groups should not become permanent, however, or they may isolate English language learners from the rest of the class.

SHARE AND RESPECT CULTURE

You can show respect for the language and culture of your students by making it visible in the classroom. English language learners can become a resource for teaching other students about language and language learning.

One important way for you to support and respect your students' culture is to use multicultural books (in which the main characters are members of a particular culture) or bilingual books (which are written in two different languages). Research shows that children better remember and comprehend books that have characters from their native cultures (Drucker, 2003). Publishers now produce a wide assortment of children's books in other languages and bilingual books. A list of multicultural books for ELL students can be found in Figure 8.3.

■ **Figure 8.3**   Multicultural Books for ELL Students

Asian

Barry, David. (1994). *The Rajah's Rice: A Mathematical Folktale from India.* Scientific America Books for Young Readers (picture book).

Choi, Sook Nyui. (1991). *Year of Impossible Goodbyes.* Houghton (chapter book).

Dooley, Norah. (1991). *Everybody Cooks Rice.* Carolroda (picture book).

Friedman, Ina. (1984). *How My Parents Learned to Eat.* Houghton (picture book).

Lee, Marie. (1993). *If It Hadn't Been for Yoon Jun.* Houghton Mifflin (chapter book).

Levin, Ellen. (1989). *I Hate English.* Scholastic (picture book).

Levine, Arthur. (1994). *The Boy Who Drew Cats: A Japanese Folktale.* Dial (picture book).

Lord, Bette Bao. (1984). *In the Year of the Boar and Jackie Robinson.* Harper (chapter book).

Mochizuki, Ken. (1993). *Baseball Saved Us.* Lee and Low (picture book).

Morimoto, Junko. (1990). *My Hiroshima.* Viking (picture book).

Nam, Vickie. (2001). *Yell-oh Girls: Emerging Voices Explore Culture, Identity, and Growing Up Asian American.* Dial.

Ness, Caroline & Neil Philip. (1996). *The Ocean of Story: Fairy Tales from India.* Lothrop, Lee & Shepard (picture book).

Newton, Patricia. (1990). *The Stonecutter: An Indian Folktale.* Putnam (picture book).

Nhuong, Huynh Quang. (1982). *The Land I Lost: Adventures of a Boy in Vietnam.* Harper (chapter book).

Rattigan, Jama Kim. (1993). *Dumpling Soup.* Little (picture book).

Sakai, Kimiko. (1990). *Sachiko Means Happiness.* Children's Book Press (picture book).

Salisbury, Graham. (1994). *Under the Blood-Red Sun.* Delacorte (chapter book).

Say, Allen. (1993). *Grandfather's Journey.* Houghton (picture book).

Shepard, Aaron. (1995). *The Gifts of Wali Dad: A Tale of India and Pakistan.* Atheneum (picture book).

So-un, Kim. (2004). *Korean Children's Favorite Stories.* Tuttle Publishing (picture book).

Uchida, Yoshiko. (1993). *Journey to Topaz.* Atheneum (chapter book).

Latino

Aardema, Verna. (1991). *Borreguita and Coyote.* Knopf (picture book).

Anaya, Rudolfo. (1998). *Farolitos for Abuelo.* Hyperion (picture book).

Brusca, Maria. (1995) *Pedro Fools the Gringo and Other Tales of a Latin American Trickster.* Holt. (picture book).

Carlson, Lori. (1994). *Bilingual Poems on Growing Up Latino in the United States.* Holt (poetry).

Cofer, Judith. (2003). *Riding Low on the Streets of Gold: Latino Literature for Young Adults.* Arte Publico Press (chapter book).

Delacre, Lulu. (1989). *Arroz con Leche: Popular Songs and Rhymes from Latin America.* NY: Scholastic (poetry).

Gerson, Mary-Joan. (1995). *People of Corn: A Mayan Story.* Little Brown (picture book).

Gerson, Mary-Joan. (2001). *Fiesta Femenina: Celebrating Women in Mexican Folktale.* Barefoot Books (picture books).

Gnojewski, Carol. (2003). *Cinco de Mayo: Celebrating Hispanic Pride.* Berkeley Heights, NJ: Enslow Publishers (picture book).

Gonzalez, Lucia. (1999). *The Bossy Gallito.* Scholastic (bilingual picture book).

Osa, Nancy. (2003). *Cuba 15: A Novel.* Delacourte Press (chapter book).

Pitre, Felix. (1993). *Juan Bobo and the Pig.* Lodestar (picture book).

San Souci, Robert. (1998). *Cendrillon: A Caribbean Cinderella.* Simon & Schuster (picture book).

Soto, Gary. (1993). *Too Many Tamales.* Putnam (picture book).

Soto, Gary. (1995). *Chato's Kitchen.* Putnam (picture book).

Middle Eastern

Al-Windawi, Thura. 2004. *Thura's Diary.* Viking (chapter book).

Hickox, Rebecca. (1998). *The Golden Sandal: A Middle Eastern Cinderella.* Holiday House (picture book).

Kimmel, Eric. (1994). *The Three Princes: A Tale from the Middle East.* Holiday House (picture book).

Nye, Naomi. (2002). *19 Varieties of Gazelle: Poems of the Middle East.* Greenwillow Books (poetry).

Staples, Suzanne. (1989). *Shabana: Daughter of the Wind.* Knopf (chapter book).

You also can promote cultural sharing through students' writing. Padano (1998) reports on a middle school where students bring in pictures of their families and their neighborhoods so that they can write about them. Such writing allows students to take pride in their families and culture, and it is highly contextualized because the people and places that students are writing about are right before their eyes.

☐ INTERVENTIONS WHEN STUDENTS STRUGGLE

Many ELL students do just fine in their classes and are able to quickly learn English and adapt to their environment. Other ELL students need more specific interventions to succeed. The following activities are often used with native English speakers, but they can be adapted to the needs of students who are learning English.

SHARED READING

Drucker (2003) noted that **shared reading** could be very useful for helping ELL students develop left-to-right and top-to-bottom orientation if their home language does not follow those conventions. Shared reading allows English language learners to focus on the written forms of words while simultaneously hearing them and trying to pronounce them. It is a low-risk activity because students are generally asked to read aloud only with a group or with small amounts of familiar text.

JOURNAL WRITING

Padano (1998) emphasizes ELL students writing in dialog journals with the teacher or with peers who are proficient in English. In this sort of written conversation, the English language learner can use the partner's writing as a model for spelling, syntax, and vocabulary. As a variation, Padano suggests having students correspond with students from another school or with university students.

For journal writing and other forms of writing activities, be careful not to overcorrect either punctuation or spelling. First focus on and correct only those mistakes that are easy to fix and affect meaning. Wilhelm (2004) gives his ELL students "grammar gifts" by modeling responses to their writing.

SHARED WRITING

Just as shared reading can support English language learners as they read, **language experience activities (LEA)** and **interactive writing** can support their writing. In LEA, the teacher provides a common experience such as a field trip, a demonstration, or a short video and then invites students to dictate sentences about the experience. The teacher may act as a scribe or coach while students write the sentences on chart papers. The texts that are created can be displayed as models for additional writing or for further instruction in reading.

SHELTERED INSTRUCTION

English language learners will need additional attention in academic reading situations. Burke (2004) generated a list of content-area vocabulary and helped his ELL students use it to write essay answers on tests. Herrell & Jordan (2004) suggests the use of **sheltered instruction,** a modified curriculum for ELL students in the content areas.

You will need to take special care to activate prior knowledge and cultural context before reading. This may have to be extended for ELL students through pictures, videos, role-playing, and so forth. You will also want to pre-view texts to identify unfamiliar words to teach.

STRATEGY TEACHING

Explicit teaching of strategies is important for all students, but may be especially important with English language learners. Padano (1998) points out that many English language learners, like less-proficient English speakers, tend to believe that they cannot understand the sentences they are reading if they encounter an unfamiliar word. Explicit instruction shows them how to use strategies such as rereading and reading ahead to help them figure out the unfamiliar word rather than giving up. In a large-scale study with 254 ELL fifth-graders, Carlo, August, McLaughlin, Snow, Lippman, and White (2004) found that students who are taught explicit word identification strategies showed significant improvement in their English reading ability.

OTHER SUGGESTIONS

- Keep a file of pictures to help communicate with ELL students and to teach them key words such as *bathroom*. You can also help students create a picture dictionary (Herrel & Jordan, 2004).
- Do not overemphasize correct pronunciation at first and never embarrass students in front of their peers.
- In the beginning, ask questions that require either a yes or no or a one- to three-word response.
- As much as possible, work one on one with students.
- Use highly predictable books with a clear language pattern for beginning readers.

☐ NONMAINSTREAM ENGLISH SPEAKERS

For teachers, differences in the dialects of English that students use can become a complex issue. Language is an important part of a person's identity. Teachers must be careful to respect the language that students bring to the classroom and to build on it as a way of extending their ability to communicate. Language also does a great deal to define and influence a person's relationships with other individuals and with the larger society. Some forms and uses of language may be typical of a majority, or mainstream, culture, while other forms that are equally valid may be used only in certain regions or by minority cultures.

Language arts teachers need to understand the characteristics of dialects. They also need instructional practices that will help students develop literacy abilities that will allow them to meet their personal, social, and economic goals.

The term **standard English** is sometimes used to describe the dialect spoken by the majority culture, but it may be more accurate to say that standard English is the language that is used in relatively formal spoken and written situations. Almost all English speakers also use "nonstandard" forms in their oral language interactions with friends and family.

Many African-American students, especially ones in urban areas, speak a form of nonmainstream English commonly called African-American vernacular English (AAVE) or **black English vernacular (BEV).** Since BEV differs consistently from the formal language of standard English, it can be considered a nonmainstream form of speech.

BEV is also known as **ebonics** (a portmanteau of *ebony* and *phonics*). In 1996, the Oakland California School Board passed a resolution acknowledging ebonics as a separate language in an attempt to receive additional funding for their schools. As a result, a backlash erupted criticizing the school board and scoffing at the notion that ebonics was more than poor or lazy grammar.

Since this time, BEV has been widely studied. In 1997, the Linguistic Society of America described ebonics as a "systematic and rule-governed" language variant spoken by many African-Americans (Gupta, 2000). Figure 8.4 describes the phonological and grammatical features of BEV.

The use of nonmainstream English in the classroom remains a controversial issue in America. On the one hand, BEV is part of many African-Americans' cultural heritage. It is the language they grew up hearing and is part of their group identity. "If teachers label their language as wrong, we are not only undermining their confidence and criticizing their culture, we are confusing them in their growing understanding of language" (Gupta, 2000). On the other hand, mainstream formal English is the language of higher education

■ FIGURE 8.4   Black English Vernacular

Feature	Example
Intial /th/ can become /d/	*them = dem*
Final /th/ becomes /f/	*with = wif*
Final consonant clusters are reduced	*ask = axe*
Deletion of /r/ after a vowel	*door = doe*
Substituting /skr/ for /str/	*street = skreet*
Short vowel substitutions	*thing = thang*
Grammar and Inflectional Endings	
Omission of verbs: *is, am, was, were*	*You out the game.*
Dropping of present tense inflections	*He fast in everything he do.*
Omission of plurals and possessives with -*s*	*I got five cent. This is Jamal book.*
Omission of past tense indicators such as -*ed*	*He talk to her.*
Use of double negatives	*He don't know nothing.*

Source: Adapted from Daniels, E. B. (1992). *Black communications: Breaking the barriers.* Chicago: New Press.

and corporate America. If students are going to succeed in life, they will most likely need to use mainstream English.

Many successful African-American students have learned to do **code-switching.** That is, speaking a mainstream English in the classroom and other formal situations, and using a nonmainstream dialect with friends in informal situations. It is important to note that all people engage in code-switching when they find themselves changing from informal to formal contexts. Think of how you would speak differently at a party with friends than teaching in front of a classroom of students.

CULTURALLY RESPONSIVE INSTRUCTION

Teachers are in a particularly sensitive position when it comes to nonmainstream language in the classroom, especially since the majority of teachers in the United States come from white, middle-class backgrounds. If teachers constantly attempt to correct students' speech in front of their peers, they will likely resent it and tune out. A better approach is **culturally responsive instruction,** which views nonmainstream dialects through a **difference orientation** rather than a deficit one (Christian, 2000). In this approach, teachers uncritically acknowledge nonmainstream English, and at the same time actively teach formal, standard English.

Sanacore (2004) states that genuine caring and respect for African-American children is the key to their literacy learning. In fact, Hornick (2000) states that positive teacher attitudes are the most important factor in helping students learn mainstream English. Some of the best strategies for teaching mainstream English in a culturally responsive way are as follows:

- Work with students privately, in nonjudgmental ways. Do not correct speech during student presentations, or in a way that might embarrass students in front of peers.
- Create "bilingual" dictionaries and wall charts of standard and nonstandard words and phrases (Gupta, 2000; Delpit, 1997).
- Ignore oral reading miscues due to nonmainstream speech unless they interfere with the meaning of the text.
- Use role-playing to practice code-switching. Gupta (2000) suggests having "formal days" where students dress up and practice using mainstream English.
- Use drama to practice oral language. Sanacore (2004) suggests a readers theatre as a great way to do this.
- Tape-record students speaking. Some teachers have found that by listening to their own tapes, students begin to code-switch to mainstream English (Delpit, 1997).
- Do daily writing in nonthreatening ways such as writing workshop and dialogue journals. Gupta (2000) suggests teaching writing conventions using a "morning message."
- Use multicultural literature with dialects. Students will see that there is a place for different forms of English.
- Have students participate in cooperative learning groups. Sanacore (2004) says that using literature circles is an effective way to encourage oral discussion.

Teaching students to write standard English is a much greater challenge than teaching oral language. Hornick (2000) found that substantial practice, writing for personally significant purposes, and writing for multiple audiences was the most effective way to teach older students who used nonstandard English. In a comparison study (Fogel & Ehri, 2000) of three groups of third- and fourth-grade students who used nonstandard English, the group that was taught story exposure, received rules for standard English, and was given guided writing practice showed the most gains in their writing.

REGIONAL DIALECTS

Black English vernacular is certainly not the only dialect in the United States. You might think, because of the common influence of radio and television, that all Americans have begun to sound alike. Across the country, however, people have retained their regional speech. Southerners really do sound different than Northerners. Walt Wolfram (2000), who has done an extensive study of dialects, recommends that students study various dialects, to learn more about English. He states:

> In fact, a respect for a dialect variation and the roles different dialects play in American society should encourage students to use standard English for its socially justified, pragmatic reasons. (p. 1)

A look at the differences in word pronunciations around the country can be fascinating. Figure 8.5 illustrates many of the common regional dialects.

To learn more about phonics and word identification, students need to feel welcome in the classroom and secure enough to use the language they have as they try to learn new language forms and skills. Classrooms accommodate language differences best when students have frequent opportunities for interacting with peers, for self-expression, and for exploring their own culture and those of others. Activities such as readers and writers workshops, shared reading, and interactive writing allow teachers to meet a wide range of language differences.

BEFORE YOU MOVE ON

Check Your Understanding

Review the main ideas from this chapter by completing the following reaction guide.

Mark + if you agree that an idea was stated in this chapter or

Mark − if you believe that it was not.

_____English language learners may have become proficient in understanding and using *conversational English*, but still struggle with *academic English*, the language used in teaching and in textbooks.

_____Students should not be asked to speak or write in English to avoid causing embarrassment.

_____Language that must be understood apart from the person who produced it and the situation in which it was created is *decontextualized*, which makes it harder to understand.

_____*Ebonics*, or *Black English vernacular*, is not a separate language. Like a language, it is systematic and rule governed.

_____Individuals who speak *nonmainstream English* generally learn *code-switching* to succeed in the majority culture.

_____Culturally *responsive teaching* includes treating oral reading miscues that occur due to nonstandard speech as a *difference* rather than a *deficit*, so the teacher should ignore these errors unless they interfere with the meaning of the text.

Maine/Northern New England
- Characterized by clipped speech
- May add an /r/ to the end of words: idear, tunar
- Specialized words like *nor'easter* (meaning a bad storm), *mackerel sky* (cloud patterns that look like a fish)

Boston
- Dropping the /r/ sound: "Park the car in Harvard yard" sounds like "Pahk the cah in Hahvahd yahd"

New York City
- R-controlled vowels interchanged: *third* becomes thoid
- /th/ becomes /d/: *dey* for *they*
- Cramming words together: *fugedaboudit* (forget about it)

Chicago
- *The* becomes *da* as in *Da Bulls*
- Food words: *brat* for *bratwurst* (pronounced braht), *dawg* for *hot dog*, *brewski* for *beer*, *beef* for *Italian beef sandwich*

Appalachian
- Adding *a* to beginning of verbs ending in -*ing*: *a'waitin*
- /th/ at the end of a word pronounced like /f/
- *The* often left out of sentence: "They a-celebratin' his birfday by a-goin' to thetah"

Southern
- Slower pronunciation of vowel sounds
- Short /i/ and /e/ pronounced the same: *tin* sounds the same as *ten* except when followed by a nasal /n/ as in *den*
- Long /i/ pronounced like /ah/
- /oo/ = /yoo/
- Contracting of words: *you all* = *y'all*

Louisiana
- Three dialects: Cajun French, Cajun English, French Creole
- *Un-yon* = onion, "I ga-RON-tee" = "I guarantee"
- Common greeting: "Where y'at"

Southwest/Texas
- Influence of Spanish words and pronunciation
- Different pronunciation: *agger-vated* for *aggravated*
- Specialized words: *blue norther* (a fierce storm with blue-black clouds), *frog-strangler* (an extraordinary amount of rain)

Northern, Minnesota
- Norwegian influence
- Elongated /o/
- *Ya'betcha, yah*

Southern California
- Elongated vowels: so dude

What Do You Call a Doughnut?

Boil cakes (New England)
Crullers (Hudson Valley, New York)
Fried cakes (Inland, northern states)
Bismarks (jelly doughnuts only, Upper Midwest, Rocky Mountains)
Belly Sinkers (North midland states)
Fasnacht (Pennsylvania Dutch)

Source: Adapted from Delaney, 2000.

WHAT'S IN THIS CHAPTER FOR ME?

Early Childhood Teachers

The youngest ELL students often have the easiest time transitioning between two different languages. Rapid language learning is a natural developmental task for young children, and they face fewer academic language demands, so they may "catch up" to the rest of the class fairly quickly. Teachers in the primary grades should carefully observe children's oral language interactions and create a language-rich environment where English language learners have plenty of opportunity to hear and use English in contextualized situations such as the morning message and project work in small groups.

This chapter points out how nonmainstream English speakers need supportive environments in which to succeed. Look carefully at the suggestions for creating these environments. What other ideas for instruction and assessment from this chapter are you most likely to use in your own classroom?

Middle Grade Teachers

By the middle grades, many English language learners will have acquired conversational English, but you cannot take that for granted. You will want to continually model word identification strategies that were explained in earlier chapters such as using sentence context and structural analysis.

You will want to have students write frequently, both formally and informally. Dialogue journals allow you to monitor students' ongoing improvement in using the structures and conventions of standard English. You can use information about the demands of academic language to help your students learn new vocabulary and work through differences in their background knowledge.

Students in the middle grades are extremely social and all too conscious of the opinions of others. Both English language learners and speakers of nonmainstream dialects may feel self-conscious about their language. You can help all students to use their language and to have a place in the classroom by following the guidelines in this chapter for creating supportive environments.

Intervention Specialists

Grant and Wong (2003) point out that reading specialists may know a great deal about literacy but little about the needs of English language learners. Intervention specialists may feel equally unprepared as to the needs of ELL and nonstandard English users. You may play a crucial role in determining whether a student is struggling with literacy because of language differences or because of some other learning problem.

Many of the instructional techniques described in this chapter can be highly effective interventions. Language experience activities and interactive writing, for example, can be adapted to a wide range of situations where students need a "bridge" between their spoken language and written English.

APPENDIX

COMPUTER SOFTWARE

☐ WEBSITES FOR KIDS WITH SPECIAL NEEDS

www.Idonline.org/kidzone/kidzone.html

This is a wonderful website for kids with learning disabilities, "where kids can play and learn." One of the best features is an online magazine where kids can submit their own writing and artwork and read other kids' work. There is an art gallery of kids' work, an annotated list of books that kids will find interesting and readable, and lots of fun activities for kids. The website also has a more serious side. It gives kids helpful, clearly written learning strategies. Also on this site are excellent resources for parents and teachers including articles, a free newsletter, and an online "Ask the Expert" feature.

www.edbydesign.com

This is a website for "kids of all abilities." It features educational activities for kids ages 5 to 16, including math games, scrambled puzzles, Harry Potter features, and a section that publishes children's stories online. There are "special needs software" programs especially for children with autism and Down syndrome, and a "special needs corner" for kids with intellectual disabilities that features a variety of art ideas and "very special home pages" of people with disabilities. There are also some excellent parent and teacher resources on this website.

cdc.gov/ncbdd/kids/kidhome.htm

This site is a KidsQuest on disabilities and health designed for students in fourth to sixth grade to ask questions and find information about kids with disabilities. The quest consists of 10 steps in which students first take an "attitude checkup" to discover their beliefs about students with special needs such as learning, physical, behavioral, or mental disabilities. The students are clearly directed to discover more information about students with special needs by linking them to related sites, such as a comic strip written by a person in a wheelchair, and challenging the students to create projects, such as checking their own environment for barriers and designing an accessible school bathroom. At the end of the quest, students retake the attitude checkup and discover how their own knowledge and beliefs about special needs students have changed.

☐ WRITING AND SPELLING SOFTWARE

WRITING EMPHASIS

KID PIX DELUX 3 (2000) THE LEARNING COMPANY

This program includes not only a word-processing program but also a graphics program, "Paint Zone," to illustrate the students' writing. Students can create a professional-looking movie slide show in which they can add animation, sounds, and Quick Time Video clips. With the voice recognition software, students can "teach" the computer to recognize proper names and other specialized words.

FAIRY TALE AND COMIC BOOK MAKER (2001) VISIONS TECHNOLOGY IN EDUCATION

Using this program, students can create a comic book with a fairy-tale theme using lifelike background scenes. They can use stock characters or create their own. Students produce the layouts of individual cells on a page; then play back the entire book using animation and sound. They can even supply the voice of each character.

ULTIMATE WRITING AND CREATIVITY CENTER (1997) RIVERDEEP INTERACTIVE LEARNING LIMITED

Students trying to write a story can receive help from "Writing Ideas Land" and the character, Penny. They can also add art and objects to their writing, and interesting information by accessing "Get the Facts." Once the story is complete, it can be seen and heard in "Presentation Theatre."

STORYBOOK WEAVER DELUXE (1997) MATTEL

The program features a word-processing program, graphics library, and paint program, as well as a thesaurus. Students can get inspiration from "Story Starter Ideas" and choose from many sophisticated foregrounds, backgrounds, and sound effects. It also has a sound playback feature.

KID WORKS 2 (1992) DAVIDSON

Even the youngest students can use this kid-friendly word-processing and paint program. It provides picture icons for some words, as well as sound effects and voice recognition playback.

My First Amazing Diary (2000) D. K. Publishing

This kid-friendly program uses picture icons that lead students through steps and questions to create diary entries. Topics include "This Is Me," "When I Was Small," and "My Family Portrait." The accompanying teacher notebook has excellent ties to curriculum and standards.

Spelling Emphasis

I Love Spelling (1997) Irvin Publishing

Students can play on three levels of spelling difficulty on three "planets" using an outerspace theme. On the planet "Anagrama" students must rearrange the letters of a word into their correct order. They are given 1000 points to begin, and can buy a clue for 10 points. Teachers can access students' scores and check their progress.

Carmen Sandiego: Word Detective (1997) Broderbund

This program is a variation of the popular social studies game, and features the spy, Carmen, who must stop the bad guys in various exciting situations. In one game, henchmen have stolen the letters from words, and players must type in the missing letters. They can use a "rule lever" for additional help. A nice feature of this program is the ability to enter a custom spelling list and to play under three levels of difficulty.

Spelling Blaster (1996) Knowledge Adventure

In this program, players must identity which alien character has stolen the missing books by playing games that identify misspelled words or supplying missing letters. Players collect clues to help eliminate each of the suspects, and find the guilty one. The default word list consists of only phonetically regular words, but can be customized with your own words or ones chosen from a word bank of 700 words. The "galactic" characters in this program are cute, but seem out of date.

☐ Spelling Websites

Websites can easily become obsolete on today's rapidly changing worldwide web. These are a few selected sites that appear to be long lasting, but to explore more current sites, do a keyword search of "spelling instruction." Look for sites that would be helpful to teachers at a specific grade level. Do the sites give specific, research-based ideas on the best ways to teach spelling? Are there helpful features that you could use with a class or a small group such as games, worksheets, or test generators using your own spelling words? Now look for sites that your students could use. Are the sites clearly explained in age-appropriate language? Are there interactive games or activities in which the students type in answers and get a response? Would students really learn from the activities, or is the emphasis on the game itself? For more websites, go to the Companion Website.

www.funbrain.com/spell and *www.funbrain.com/spellroo*

These twin sites are geared to teachers and are chock full of spelling exercises and activities for grades 1 through 8. Spelling lists for each of these grade levels can be downloaded and used with the special features on the site. The "Workout Room" has different ways to use spelling words such as in puzzles, in the context of current events ("Words in the News"), in writing prompts for thank you notes, recipes, and so on, and in interesting "language facts." The "Reference Room" has wonderful teacher resources such as lists of frequently misspelled words, links to websites and online dictionaries, and spelling strategies appropriate for each developmental level. The "research" sections give short, easy-to-read explanations of current findings regarding which words are best taught as spelling words.

www.factmonster.com

This helpful site for students gives good practical advice in "10 Tips for Better Spelling," and tackles difficult spelling patterns such as *–sede* versus *–cede* in words such as *recede, proceed*, and *supersede*. There is a "spelling bee" feature where students must figure out if a word is spelled incorrectly and can click on "Need a Hint?" for help.

www.spellingbee.com

This is the official website for the Scripps-Howard Spelling Bee, and is of interest for both teachers and students. Serious spellers can learn the procedures for entering the contest, and others can view the "word of the day" and download lists of past spelling words such as these tongue-twisters that were recent winners' final words: *pococurante* and *chiaroscurist*.

GLOSSARY

Accent or **stress:** multiple syllable words receive different accents, that is, some syllables are said louder than the others. These syllables are marked in the dictionary with an accent mark

Affixes: prefixes or suffixes added to a root word

Alphabetic knowledge: knowing that letters represent sounds and that speech can be written down

Alphabetic stage: developmental word stage in which students write a letter for each sound heard, usually kindergarten through first grade

Analytical approach (to phonics): in this method, students break down the sounds of a known word such as *red* and then find other words with the same components, such as the short /e/ sound in *bet*

Automatic stage: at this developmental word stage, students can instantly recognize most of the words they encounter in print and can focus on their most important job of comprehending the text

Automaticity: ability to recall words effortlessly and fluently

Balanced literacy: a whole-part-whole instructional framework; the goal is to develop independent readers and writers by balancing direct skills instruction with authentic reading and writing

Black English vernacular (BEV): a form of nonmainstream English; also called ebonics

Blending: putting sounds together to form a whole word

Bound morphemes: ones that only have meaning when attached to a root, such as *un-* and *-ness*

Breve: diacritical marking for short vowel sounds

Buddy study: a format for spelling instruction that takes advantage of the motivating effects of working with a peer and allows for a more individualized approach to spelling

Chunking word wall: a type of a word wall in which a key word is chosen to represent each common rime chunk. For example, *ran* might go on a chunking word wall to represent the *-an* rime. These words can be used to compare and contrast new words with the same chunk, such as *than* or *banana*

Closed syllable: a syllable that ends in a consonant

Code-switching: speaking a mainstream English in the classroom and other formal situations, and using a nonmainstream dialect with friends in informal situations

Cognates: words that are written or pronounced almost the same in two different languages

Compound words: a combination of two free morphemes

Consolidated stage: developmental word stage in which students use their experience in reading and writing chunks of words and expand it to include prefixes, suffixes, and other affixes

Consonant blend: see *consonant cluster*

Consonant cluster: two or more consonant letters that blend together when sounded, more commonly called *consonant blends*

Consonant digraphs: two-letter combinations that make only one sound

Cues or **cueing systems:** information that all readers use to understand text; the three basic cueing systems are graphophonemic, semantic, and syntactic

Cultural abandonment: the conflict that English language learners may feel between taking on a new culture and respecting their native culture

Culturally responsive instruction: approach in which teachers uncritically acknowledge nonmainstream English, and at the same time, actively teach formal, standard English

Decodable text: very simple text that employs primarily words that are phonetically regular

Decoding by analogy or **compare/contrast:** comparing known word with new ones not by looking at individual letters, but at the familiar patterns of letters (*back-smacked*)

Decontextualized: taken out of a familiar context making something harder to understand

Developmental delays: used to describe students with IQs below 85

Diacritical marks: used to show vowel sounds to aid pronunciation

Difference orientation: an approach that views the use of nonmainstream dialects such as BEV as a result of differences, rather than deficits

Dyslexia: a severe form of reading disability

Ebonics: a form of nonmainstream English; also referred to as African-American vernacular English (AAVE) or black English vernacular (BEV)

Embedded approach: teaching phonics skills within the context of real literature

Environmental print: print from the surrounding environment such as a McDonald's sign or a stop sign that young children often recognize before formal reading

Free morphemes: word parts that have meaning on their own, such as *happy* in *unhappy*

Function words: common words that cannot easily be defined, such as *of, the,* or *was*

Graphemes: written representation of phoneme sounds; they are usually single letters, but can be more than one letter, such as *th*, because *th* represents only one sound as in *think*

Graphophonemic cueing system: associating letters with sounds to decode words

Guided reading groups: working with students in small groups using leveled texts to develop reading strategies

High frequency words or **sight words:** the most common words in the English language that should be instantly recalled

Hink pinks: a pair of rhyming words that serve as the answer to a riddle (*nice ice*)

Idioms: phrases with a specialized meaning in a language (*easy as pie*)

Inflectional endings: endings added to words that change the grammatical structure of the word (*-ing, -est*)

Informal reading inventory (IRI): assessment consisting of reading passages written at increasingly higher grade levels that can be used to identify miscues and cue use; questions are supplied to check comprehension and both fiction and nonfiction passages are included. Both oral and silent reading are assesed

Interactive writing or **shared writing:** a format in which students are actively involved in producing a piece of writing. This often involves "sharing the pen" when writing a text

Invented spelling: The kind of writing that students often do in the phonemic and transitional stages of spelling development using letters to represent sounds, i.e., *lik* for *lick* or *like*

Language Experience Activities (LEA): format for teaching reading by using the child's own dictated language as a text and basis for instruction

Letter knowledge: being able to identify the letters of the alphabet out of order

Leveled texts: books that have been identified as being on a particular developmental reading level

Literature circles: small heterogeneous groups of students who come together to discuss a book that they have all read

Macron: diacritical mark for a long vowel sound

Mini lessons: short, focused lessons designed to directly and systematically teach those skills all students will need when they are reading

Morpheme: the smallest unit of meaning in a word (*un* or *happy* in *unhappy*)

Morphemic analysis: breaking down words into meaningful units to understand their meaning

Onsets: letters that come before a vowel in a syllable

Open syllables: syllables that end in a vowel

Orthographic knowledge: knowing the spelling of common letter patterns

Orthography: how graphemes are arranged into identifiable patterns in a language, in other words, spelling

Oxymorons: two words that appear to contradict each other, such as *bittersweet* and *cruel kindness*

Palindromes: words or phrases that are spelled the same backwards and forwards

Partial alphabetic stage: in this word developmental stage children, usually from kindergarten to beginning first grade, know most of the letter names and the sounds of most consonants, along with some vowel sounds, usually the short ones

Phoneme: the smallest unit of sound in a language represented, for example, as /b/

Phonemic awareness: being able to distinguish and manipulate phonemes in spoken words; concerned only with sounds, not letters

Phonetic or **temporary spelling:** more useful terms for invented spelling since they reflect the developmental nature of spelling

Phonics: the knowledge about letters, sounds, and words that people use to create meaning when reading and writing and the ways in which they are guided to acquire that knowledge

Phonograms or **word families:** rime chunks that can generate many rhyming words

Portmanteaus: words that are shortened from two words (*brunch* from *breakfast* and *lunch*)

Prealphabetic stage: children at this stage, usually from preschool to kindergarten, do not have alphabetic knowledge; they do not associate letters with sounds and may not know the concept of a word

Prefix: a morpheme added at the beginning of a root word

Primary language: the first or home language spoken

Prompt: a topic or question provided by the teacher to direct student writing. An example might be, "Write about a time when you were afraid."

Respelling: phonetic spelling of a word in a dictionary used to show how it is pronounced

Rime: the vowel and the rest of the letters in a syllable, also called a *chunk* or *phonogram*

Running records: a systematic method for assessing how young students monitor their own reading using a shorthand method of recording oral reading

Schwa: nondistinct vowel sound in an unaccented syllable

Segmenting: breaking down a word into the individual sounds of letters (*s-a-t*)

Semantic cueing system: cues that use meaning—from the sentence context, the pictures, the reader's background knowledge, and so forth

Shared reading: a method of teaching beginning reading, often using an enlarged text such as a Big Book, to involve students in a text that they would not be able to read independently

Shared writing or **interactive writing:** format in which students are actively involved in producing a piece of writing

Sheltered instruction: a modified curriculum for ELL students in the content areas

Spelling approach: a method that teaches phonics through spelling instruction

Standard English: written English that conforms to mainstream rules and conventions

Standards: explicit statements that identify what all students on a particular grade level should know and be able to do

Standards-based education: a system for using standards for developing curriculum and assessment

Structural analysis: the process of breaking down words to understand their meaning and to learn their spelling

Suffix: a morpheme; and a type of affix that is added to the end of a word

Syllable: a basic unit of pronunciation, and as such, can only contain one vowel phoneme

Syntactic cueing system: knowledge about "grammar," the ways in which words can and cannot be put together in a particular language

Synthetic phonics: individually sounding out the letter sounds and then blending those sounds into words

Transfer words: longer, more difficult words that contain the same chunks as the targeted words. For example, "stranded" for -and

Visual configurations: the outline shape of words

Vowel digraphs: two-letter vowel combinations that represent only one vowel phoneme (*oo*)

Vowel diphthong: a single vowel phoneme that is written with two letters that resemble a gliding sound between the vowel sounds (*oi, ow*)

Word identification: the process of determining the pronunciation and some degree of meaning of an unknown word

Word ladder: an activity designed to help students practice reading and spelling. The teacher dictates a word, then gives clues to the next word—which has only a one or two letter difference. For example, the first word might be *snow* and the second word might be *show*. Students write the words until they come to a final word with a very different meaning. In this case, *snow* is eventually turned into *rain*

Word sorts: classifying words into different categories—closed sorts have categories determined by the teacher; open sorts are determined by the students

Word wall: a display of words on a classroom wall designed to help students with their reading and writing. A high frequency word wall features the most common words in English that students are expected to read and spell instantly. Chunking word walls have key words that contain common rime chunks such as *-an*. Students use these words to compare with others containing the same chunk

Writing journals: notebooks in which students practice writing and spelling daily

Writing workshop: classroom organization plan designed to emphasize the process of writing in a more authentic way; individual student writing is done in five general but not strictly sequential steps

REFERENCES

Adams, M. (1990). *Beginning to read: Thinking and learning about print.* Cambridge, MA: MIT Press.

Allen, J. (2003). But they still can't (or won't) read! Helping children overcome roadblocks to reading. *Language Arts, 80*(4), 268–273.

Allen, V. G. (1994). Selecting materials for reading instruction of ESL children. In K. Spangenberg-Urbschat & R. Pritchard (Eds.), *Kids come in all languages: Reading instruction for ESL students.* Newark, DE: IRA.

Barr, R. C. (1972). The influence of instructional conditions on word recognition errors. *Reading Research Quarterly, 7,* 509–529.

Bartlett, B. (2002). Sounds like an alphabet. *The Reading Teacher, 55*(5), 474.

Baumann, J. F., Hoffman, J. V., Moon, J., & Duffy-Hester, A. M. (1998). Where are teachers' voices in the phonics/whole language debate? Results from a survey of U. S. elementary classroom teachers. *The Reading Teacher, 51*(8), 636–650.

Bear, D. R., Invernizzi, M., Templeton, S., & Johnson, F. (2004). *Words their way* (3rd ed.). Upper Saddle River, NJ: Merrill.

Beckham-Hungler, D., & Williams, C. (2003). Teaching words that students misspell: Spelling instruction and young children's writing. *Language Arts, 80*(4), 299–309.

Bond, G. L., & Dykstra, R. (1967). The cooperative research program in first-grade reading instruction. *Reading Research Quarterly, 2,* 1–142.

Bradley, L., & Bryant, P. (1983). Categorizing sounds and learning to read: A casual connection. *Nature, 30,* 419–421.

Brown, K. J. (1999/2000). What kind of text—for whom and when? Textual scaffolding for beginning readers. *The Reading Teacher, 53*(4), 292–307.

Brown, K. J., Sinatra, G. M., & Wagstaff, J. M. (1997). Exploring the potential of analogy instruction to support students' spelling development. *The Elementary School Journal, 97*(1), 81–98.

Bruck, M. (1992). Persistence of dyslexic's phonological awareness deficits. *Developmental Psychology, 28,* 874–886.

Burke, J. (2004). Learning the language of academic study. *Voices from the Middle, 11*(4), 37–42.

Calfee, R. (1998). Phonics and phonemes: Learning to decode and spell in a literature-based program. In J. L. Mesala & L. Ehri (Eds.), *Word recognition in beginning Literacy* (pp. 315–340). Mahwah, NJ: L. Erlbaum Associates.

Cantrell, S. C. (1999). Effective teaching and literacy learning: A look inside primary classrooms. *The Reading Teacher, 52*(4), 370–378.

Carlo, M. S., August, D., McLaughlin, B., Snow, C., Lippman, D., & White, C. (2004). Closing the gap: Addressing the vocabulary needs of English-language learners in bilingual and mainstream classrooms. *Reading Research Quarterly, 39*(2), 188–215.

Chall, J. (1967). *Learning to read: The great debate.* New York: McGraw-Hill.

Chamot, A. U., & O'Malley, M. J. (1994). Instructional approaches and teaching procedures. In K. Spangenberg-Urbschat & R. Pritchard (Eds.), *Kids come in all languages: Reading instruction for ESL students.* Newark, DE: IRA.

Christian, D. (2000). Vernacular dialects in U.S. schools (ERIC Document Reproduction Service No. EED406846).

Clay, M. M. (2000). *Running records for classroom teachers.* Portsmouth, NJ: Heinemann.

Cooter, K. S., & Cooter, R. B. (2004). One size doesn't fit all: slow learners in the reading classroom. *Issues in Urban Literacy,* 680–684.

Cumins, J. (1994). The acquisition of English as a second language. In K. Spangenberg-Urbschat & R. Pritchard (Eds.), *Kids Come in All Languages: Reading Instruction for ESL Students.* Newark, DE: International Reading Association.

Cunningham, P. M. (2000). *Phonics they use.* New York: Longman.

Daniels, E. B. (1992). *Black communications: Breaking the barriers.* Chicago: New Press.

Daniels, H. (2002). *Literature circles* (2nd ed.). Portland, MN: Stenhouse Publishers.

Dank, M. E. (1976). A study of the relationship of miscues to the mode of formal reading instruction received by selected second graders. Unpublished doctoral dissertation, University of Massachusetts (ERIC Document Reproduction Service No. ED 126 431).

Delaney, R. (2000). A dialect map of American English. Retrieved June 16, 2004, from uta.fi/FAST/USI/REF/dial-/map.html.

Delpit, L. (1997). Ebonics and culturally responsive instruction. Retrieved June 14, 2004, from *Rethinking Schools Online, 12*(1), rethinkingschools.org.

Drucker, M. J. (2003). What reading teachers should know about ESL learners. *The Reading Teacher, 57*(1), 22–29.

Ehri, L., & Stahl, S. A. (2001). Beyond the smoke and mirrors: Putting out the fire. *Phi Delta Kappan, 83*(1), 17–20.

Ehri, L. C. (1998). Grapheme-phoneme knowledge is essential for learning to read words in English. In J. L. Mesala & L. C. Ehri (Eds.), *Word recognition in beginning literacy* (pp. 3–39). Mahwah, NJ: Lawrence Erlbaum Associates.

Entrikin, D., York, R., & Brown, L. (1977). Teaching trainable-level multiple handicapped students using picture cues, context cues, and initial consonant sounds to determine the labels of unknown words. *American Association for the Education of Severely/Profoundly Handicapped Review, 2,* 169–190.

Fawcett, A., & Nicolson, R. (1995). Persistence of phonological awareness deficits in older children with dyslexia. *Reading and Writing: An Interdisciplinary Journal, 7,* 361–376.

Fernald, G. M. (1988). *Remedial techniques in basic subjects.* Austin, TX: Pro-Ed.

Fogel, H., & Ehri, L. C. (2000). Teaching elementary students who speak black English vernacular to write in standard English: Effects of dialect transformation practice.

Fountas, I. C., & Pinnell, G. S. (1996). *Guided Reading.* Portsmouth, NH: Heinemann.

Fox, B. J. (2003). *Word recognition activities.* Columbus, OH: Merrill Prentice Hall.

Fox, B. J., & Hull, M. A. (2002). *Phonics for the teacher of reading.* Upper Saddle River, NJ: Merrill.

Fu, D. (2004). Teaching ELL students in regular classrooms at the secondary level. *Voices from the Middle, 11*(4), 8–15.

Garan, E. M. (2001). Beyond the smoke and mirrors: A critique of the National Reading Panel report on phonics. *Phi Delta Kappan, 82*(7), 500–507.

Garcia, G. E. 1994. Assessing the literacy development of second-language students: A focus on authentic assessment. In K. Spangenberg-Urbschat & R. Pritchard (Eds.), *Kids Come in All Languages: Reading Instruction for ESL Students.* Newark, DE: International Reading Association.

Gaskins, I. (1997). Analyzing words and making discoveries about the alphabetic system: Activities for beginning readers. *Language Arts, 74*(3), 172–184.

Gaskins, I. (1998a). A beginning literacy program for at-risk and delayed readers. In J.L. Metsala & L.C. Ehri (Eds.), *Word recognition in beginning literacy* (pp. 209–231). Mahwah, NJ: Lawrence Erlbaum Associates.

Gaskins, I. (1998b). There's more to teaching at-risk and delayed readers than good reading instruction. *The Reading Teacher, 51*(7), 534–537.

Gentry, R. (2002). *The literacy map: Guiding children where they need to be 4–6.* New York: MONDO Publishing.

Gonzalez-Bueno, M. (2003). Literacy activities for Spanish-English bilingual children. *The Reading Teacher, 57*(2), 189–192.

Goodman, K. (1986). *What's whole in whole language?* Portsmouth, NH: Heinemann.

Goodman, K. S. (1985). A linguistic study of cues and miscues in reading. In H. Singer & R. B. Buddell (Eds.), *Theoretical models and processes of reading* (3rd ed., pp. 129–134). Newark, NJ: International Reading Association.

Goodman, K. S. (1992). I didn't found whole language. *The Reading Teacher, 46*(3), 188–199.

Goswami, U. (1998). The role of analogies in the development of word recognition. In J.L. Mesala & L. C. Ehri (Eds.), *Word recognition in beginning literacy* (pp. 41–63). Mahwah, NJ: Lawrence Erlbaum Associates.

Goswami, U. (2000). Phonological and lexical processes. In M. L. Kamil, P. B. Mosenthal, P. D. Pearson, & R. Barr (Eds.), *Handbook of reading research* (vol. III). Mahwah, NJ: Lawrence Erlbaum Associates.

Graham, S., & Voth, V. P. (1990). Spelling instruction: Making modifications for students with learning disabilities. *Academic Therapy, 25,* 447–457.

Grant, R. A., & Wong, S. D. (2003). Barriers to literacy for language-minority learners: An argument for change in the literacy education profession. *Journal of Adolescent & Adult Literacy, 46*(5).

Graves, M. F., Juel, C., & Graves, B. B. (1998) *Teaching reading in the 21st century.* Boston: Allyn & Bacon.

Gunning, T. G. (1995). Word building: A strategic approach to the teaching of phonics. *The Reading Teacher, 48*(6), 484–488.

Gupta, A. (2000). What's up wif Ebonics y'all? Retrieved June 16, 2004, from readingonline.org.

Hadaway, N. L., Vardell, S. M., & Young, T. A. (2001). Scaffolding oral language development through poetry for students learning English. *The Reading Teacher, 54*(8), 796–806.

Harris, T. L., & Hodges, R. E. (Eds.). (1995). *The literacy dictionary.* Newark, DE: International Reading Association.

Heilman, A. W. (2001). *Phonics in proper perspective* (9th ed.). Upper Saddle River, NJ: Merrill Prentice Hall.

Helman, L. A. (2004). Building on the sound system of Spanish: Insights from the alphabetic spellings of English-language learners. *The Reading Teacher, 57*(5), 452–460.

Helman, L. A. (2005). Using literacy assessment results to improve teaching for English-language learners. *The Reading Teacher, 58*(7), 668–677.

Henson, J., & Giles, C. (2003). Al's story: Overcoming beliefs that inhibit learning. *Language Arts, 80*(4), 259–266.

Herrell, A., & Jordan, M. (2004). *Fifty strategies for teaching English language learners (2nd ed.).* Upper Saddle River, NJ: Pearson Education.

Hickman, P., Pollard-Durodolas, & Vaughn, S. (2004). Storybook reading: Improving vocabulary and comprehension for English-language learners. *The Reading Teacher, 57*(8), 720–730.

Hornick, K. (2000). Teaching writing to linguistically diverse students (ERIC Document Reproduction Service No. ED275792).

International Reading Association (IRA). (1997). *The role of phonics in reading instruction.* Newark, DE: IRA.

International Reading Association (IRA). (1998). *Phonemic awareness and the teaching of reading.* Newark, DE: IRA.

International Reading Association (IRA). (2001). *Second language literacy instruction.* Newark, DE: IRA.

Johnson, D. D., & Baumann, J. F. (1984) Word identification. In P. D. Pearson (Ed.), *Handbook of reading research* (pp. 583–608). New York: Longman. Reading: Theory, research and practice (pp. 32–40). New York, NY: National Reading Conference.

Johnston, F. P. (2001). The utility of phonic generalizations: Let's take another look at Clymer's conclusions. *The Reading Teacher, 55*(2), 132–143.

Juel, C. (1988). Learning to read and write: A longitudinal study of fifty-four children from first through fourth grades. *Journal of Educational Psychology, 80,* 437–447.

Lesgold, A. M., & Resnick, L. B. (1982). How reading disabilities develop: Perspectives from a longitudinal study. In R. Barr, M. L. Kamil, P. Mosenthal, & P. D. Pearson (Eds.), *Handbook of reading research* (vol. II). New York: Longman.

Lindolm-Leary, K. (2000). *Biliteracy for a global society.* Washington, DC: National Clearinghouse for Bilingual Education.

Lyon, G. R. (1998). Why reading is not a natural process. *Educational Leadership, 32*(4), 13–18.

Matson, B. (1996). Whole language or phonics? Teachers and researchers find the middle ground most fetile. *The Harvard Education Letter, XII*(2), 1–3.

McCray, A. D. (2001). Middle school students with reading disabilities. *The Reading Teacher, 55*(3), 298–300.

McCrum, R., MacNeil, R., & Cran, W. (2002). *The story of English.* New York: Penguin Books.

McLaughlin, T. F., & Skinner, C. H. (1996). Improving academic performance through self-management: Cover, copy and compare. *Intervention in School and Clinic, 32,* 113–118.

Merriam Webster's Collegiate Dictionary (11th ed.). (2003). New York: Merriam-Webster.

Mesmer, H. A. (2001). Decodable text: A review of what we know. *Reading Research and Instruction, 40*(2), 121–142.

Moore, D. W., Bean, T. W., Birdyshaw, D., & Rycik, J. A. (1999). *Adolescent literacy: A position statement.* Newark, NJ: International Reading Association.

Morrow, L. M., Tracy, D. H., Woo, D. G., & Pressley, M. (1999). Characteristics of exemplary first-grade literacy instruction. *The Reading Teacher, 52*(5), 462–476.

Moustafa, M. (1997). Report card on California's reading instruction: Snatching defeat from the jaws of victory. *Los Angeles Times,* C1.

Moustafa, M., & Maldondo-Colon, E. (1999). Whole-to-parts phonics instruction: Building on what children know to help them know more. *The Reading Teacher, 52*(5), 448–458.

National Reading Panel. (2000). *Teaching children to read: An evidence based assessment of the scientific research literature on reading and its implications for reading instruction.* Washington, DC: National Institute of Child Health and Human Development.

Nilson, A. P., & Nilson, D. L. (2004). Working under lucky stars: Language lessons for multilingual classrooms. *Voices from the Middle, 11*(4), 27–32.

Norton, D. E., & Hubert, P. (1977). *A comparison of the oral reading strategies and comprehension patterns developed by high, average and low ability first grade students taught by two appraoches—phonics emphasis and eclectic basal* (ERIC Document Reproduction Service No. ED 145 393). College Station: Texas A & M University.

Ohio Department of Education. (2001). *Academic content standards.* Columbus, OH: Author.

Padano, Y. (1998). Latino students and reading: Understanding these English language learners' needs. In Beers, K. and Samules, B. G. (Eds.), *Into Focus: Understanding and Creating Middle School Readers* pp. 105–122. Norwood, MA: Christopher Gordon Publishers.

Pinnell, G. S., & Fountas, I. C. (1998). *Word matters: Teaching phonics and spelling in the reading/writing classroom.* Portsmouth NJ: Heinemann.

Polloway, C. H., & Polloway, E. A. (1981). Validation of a survival vocabulary list. *Academic Therapy, 16*, 443–448.

Polloway, E. A., Miller, L., & Smith, T. E. (2004). *Language instruction for students with disabilities.* Denver: Love Publishing.

Polloway, E. A., Polloway, J. R., & Serna, L. (2001). *Strategies for teaching learners with special needs* (7th ed.). Columbus: Merrill.

Pressley, M., Wharton-McDonald, R., Rankin, J., Mistretta, J., & Yokoi, L. (1996). The nature of outstanding primary-grades literacy instruction. In E. McIntyre & M. Pressley (Eds.), *Balanced instruction: Strategies and skills in whole language* (pp. 251–276). Mahwah, NJ: Erlbaum.

Rasinski, T., & Padak, N. (2000). *Effective reading strategies: Teaching children who find reading difficult.* Columbus, OH: Merrill.

Rasinski, T. V., & Padak, N. D. (2001). *From phonics to fluency.* New York: Longman.

Reutzel, D. R., & Cooter, R. B. (2000). *Teaching children to read.* Columbus, OH: Merrill.

Routman, R. (2000). *Conversations.* Portsmouth, NH: Heinemann.

Ruddel, R. (1995). Those influential literacy teachers: Meaning negotiation and motivation builders. *The Reading Teacher, 48*(6), 454–463.

Rupley, W. H., Logan, J. W., & Nichols, W. D. (1998/1999). Vocabulary instruction in a balanced reading program. *The Reading Teacher, 52*(4), 336–346.

Rycik J. (1997). Common sense and common ground: The appeal of balanced literacy programs. *Ohio Reading Teacher, 31*(1), 19–21.

Rycik, J. A., & Irvin, J. L. (2005). *Teaching reading in the middle grades: Understanding and supporting literacy development.* Boston: Allyn and Bacon.

Rycik, M. (2002). How primary teachers use word walls to teach literacy strategies. *The Ohio Reading Teacher, 35*(2), 13–19.

Sacks, C. H., & Mergendoller, J. R. (1997). The relationship between teachers' theoretical orientation toward reading and student outcomes in kindergarten children with different initial reading abilities. *American Educational Research Journal, 34*(4), 721–739.

Sanacore, J. (2004). Genuine caring and literacy learning for African American children. *The Reading Teacher, 57*(8), 744–753.

Share, D., Jorm, A., Maclearn, R., & Matthews. R. (1984). Sources of individual differences in reading acquisition. *Journal of Education Psychology, 76*, 1309–1324.

Shaywitz, S. (2003). *Overcoming dyslexia: A new and complete science-based program for reading problems at any level.* New York: Knopf.

Stahl, S. A. (1992). Saying the "p" word: Nine guidelines for exemplary phonics instruction. *The Reading Teacher, 45*(8), 618–625.

Stahl, S. A., Duffy-Hester, A. M., & Stahl, K. A. (1998). Everything you wanted to know about phonics (but were afraid to ask). *Reading Research Quarterly, 33*, 338–355.

Stanovich, K. E. (1991), Word recognition: Changing perspectives. In R. Barr, M. L. Kamil, P. B. Mosenthal, & P. D. Pearson (Eds.), *Handbook of reading research* (vol. 2, pp. 418–452). White Plains, NY: Longman.

Stanovich, K. E. (1993/1994). Romance and reality. *The Reading Teacher,* *47*(4) 280–291.

Strickland, D. (1998), What's basic in beginning reading. *Educational Leadership, 22,* 6–10.

Taberski, S. (2000). *On solid ground: Strategies for teaching K–3.* Portsmouth, NH: Heinemann.

Tompkins, G. E. (2006). *Literacy for the 21st century: A balanced approach.* (4th ed.) Upper Saddle River, NJ: Merrill.

Treiman, R. (1998). Why spelling? The benefits of incorporating spelling into beginning reading instruction, In J. L. Metsala & L. C. Ehri (Eds.), *Word recognition in beginning literacy* (pp. 289–313). Mahwah, NJ: Lawrence Erlbaum Associates.

Truss, L. (2003). *Eats, shoots and leaves.* New York: Penguin Books.

U.S. Department of Education. (2003). Executive summary of the No Child Left Behind Act of 2001. Available at *http://ed.gov/offices/OESE/esea/ exec-summ.html.*

Vacca, J. L., Vacca, R. T., Gove, M. K., Burkey, L., Lenhart, L. A., & McKeon, C. (2003). *Reading and learning to read* (5th ed.) Boston: Pearson.

Wagstaff, J. M. (1997/1998). Building practical knowledge of letter-sound correspondence: A beginner's word wall and beyond. *The Reading Teacher, 51*(4) 298–304.

Weaver, C. (1994). *Reading process and practice* (2nd ed.) Portsmouth, NH: Heinemann.

Wharton-McDonald, R., Pressley, M., & Mistretta-Hampston, J. (1998). Literacy instruction in nine first-grade classrooms: Teacher characteristics and student achievement. *The Elementary School Journal, 99*(2), 101–128.

Wharton-McDonald, R., Pressley, M., Rankin, J., Mistretta, J., Yokoi L., & Ettenberger, S. (1997). Effective primary grades literacy instruction=balanced literacy instruction. *The Reading Teacher, 50*(6), 518–521.

White, T. G. (2005). Effects of systematic and strategic analogy-based phonics on grade 2 students' word reading and reading comprehension. *Reading Research Quarterly, 40*(2), 234–255.

Wilhelm, J. D. (2004). Learning from ELL kids: How to teach writing. *Voices from the Middle, 11*(4), 43–44.

Wolfram, W. (2000). Incorporating dialect study into the language arts class (ERIC Document Reproduction Service No. ED318231).

Wylie, R. E., & Durrell, D. D. (1970). Teaching vowels through phonograms. *Elementary English, 47,* 787–791.

CHILDREN'S BOOKS CITED

Agee, J. (1994). *Go hang a salami: I'm a lasagna hog.* New York: Farrar, Straus, & Giroux.

Agee, J. (1994). *So many dynamos.* New York: Farrar, Straus, & Giroux.

Agee, J. (1999). *Sit on a potato pan, Otis.* New York: Farrar, Strauss, & Giroux.

Blos, J. (1979). *A gathering of days.* New York: Scribner.

Florian, D. (1988). *Insectlopedia*. New York: Scholastic.

Guarino, D. (1989). *Is your mama a llama?* New York: Scholastic.

Gwynne, F. (1970). *The king who rained*. New York: Scholastic.

Gwynne, F. (1976). *A chocolate moose for dinner*. New York: Scholastic.

Helig, K., & Hembrook D. (2002). *Mouse makes words*. New York: Scholastic.

Leedy, L., & Street, P. (2003). *There's a frog in my throat! 400 animal sayings a little bird told me*. New York: Holiday House.

Leonard, M. (1998). *I like mess*. Brookfield, CT: Millbrook Press.

Rowling, J. R. (1997). *Harry Potter and the Sorcerer's Stone*. New York: Scholastic.

Ruby, B. (1994). *Steal away home*. New York: Simon & Schuster.

Sendak, M. (1962). *Chicken soup with rice*. New York: Scholastic.

Snicket, L. (2002). *Carnivorous carnival*. New York: Scholastic.

SOFTWARE PROGRAMS

Clifford Reading. (2000). Scholastic.

Disney's Phonic Quest. (2001). Disney.

First Phonics. (1995). Sunburst.

Kids Phonics 2. (1996). Davidson.

Let's Go Read I. (1998). Edmark.

Reader Rabbit I. (2000). Learning Co.

Vowel Patterns. (2002). Tenth Planet.

Vowels Short and Long. (1999). Tenth Planet.

WEBSITES

www.americandialect.org

www.fun-with-words.com

www.janbrett.com

www.wordpowerchallenge.com

INDEX